INSIDE NEBRASKA
COURTHOUSES

DEAN B. SETTLE & HARRIET R. GROSSBART

A PROTECTOR OF JUSTICE

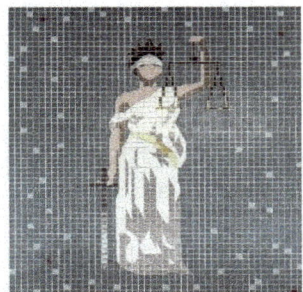

LADY JUSTICE, A SYMBOL of the American justice system, draws inspiration from the Greek goddess Themis and the Roman goddess Justitia. Her balanced scales represent fairness, acknowledging that every story has two sides in the litigation process. The blindfold signifies an impartial consideration of the facts, regardless of the litigants' race, creed or social standing. Her sword embodies the strength and authority inherent in our legal system.

BIBLIOGRAPHY

Clerk of the Legislature, "Nebraska Blue Book," 2022-23
Margaret Fletcher, "Architectural Styles: A Visual Guide," Princeton University Press, 2020
Candy Moulton, "Roadside History of Nebraska," Mountain Press Publishing Co., 1997
Diana Lambdin Meyer, "Nebraska Off the Beaten Path," Globe Pequot, 8th Edition, 2018
Nebraska Association of County Officials, "NACO County Line," December 1994
Elton A. Perkey, "Perkey's Nebraska Place Names," Nebraska State Historical Society, 1982
Oliver B. Pollak, "Nebraska Courthouses," Arcadia Publishing, 2002
William D. Rowley, "The Loup City Riot of 1934: Main Street vs. The Far-Out Left," Nebraska History, September 1966
David Hendee, "Nebraska: 150 Years Told Through 93 Counties," Omaha World-Herald, 2016
Nebraska State Historical Society, history.nebraska.gov
National Register of Historic Places – Nebraska, nationalregisterofhistoricplaces.com
Nebraska.gov, cities/counties/villages
Omaha World-Herald archives, omaha.com

On the cover: Courthouse details from Burt, Cass, Colfax, Dodge, Douglas, Fillmore, Hall, Hamilton, Johnson and Saunders counties.

ISBN 979-8-218-53706-7 Published by Dean B. Settle.
First Edition, 2024, printed by Perfection Press. Second Edition, 2025, printed by K&H Print Group. All rights reserved.
No part of this book may be reproduced without the permission of Dean B. Settle or his representatives.
www.insidenebraskacourthouses.com

NEBRASKA COUNTIES & LICENSE PLATE PREFIXES

PAGE	NAME • LICENSE PLATE PREFIX						
6	ADAMS • 14	54	DEUEL • 78	102	JOHNSON • 57	150	RED WILLOW • 48
8	ANTELOPE • 26	56	DIXON • 35	104	KEARNEY • 52	152	RICHARDSON • 19
10	ARTHUR • 91	58	DODGE • 5	106	KEITH • 68	154	ROCK • 81
12	BANNER • 85	60	DOUGLAS • 1	108	KEYA PAHA • 82	156	SALINE • 22
14	BLAINE • 86	62	DUNDY • 76	110	KIMBALL • 71	158	SARPY • 59
16	BOONE • 23	64	FILLMORE • 34	112	KNOX • 12	160	SAUNDERS • 6
18	BOX BUTTE • 65	66	FRANKLIN • 50	114	LANCASTER • 2	162	SCOTTS BLUFF • 21
20	BOYD • 63	68	FRONTIER • 60	116	LINCOLN • 15	164	SEWARD • 16
22	BROWN • 75	70	FURNAS • 38	118	LOGAN • 87	166	SHERIDAN • 61
24	BUFFALO • 9	72	GAGE • 3	120	LOUP • 88	168	SHERMAN • 56
26	BURT • 31	74	GARDEN • 77	122	MADISON • 7	170	SIOUX • 80
28	BUTLER • 25	76	GARFIELD • 83	124	McPHERSON • 90	172	STANTON • 53
30	CASS • 20	78	GOSPER • 73	126	MERRICK • 46	174	THAYER • 32
32	CEDAR • 13	80	GRANT • 92	128	MORRILL • 64	176	THOMAS • 89
34	CHASE • 72	82	GREELEY • 62	130	NANCE • 58	178	THURSTON • 55
36	CHERRY • 66	84	HALL • 8	132	NEMAHA • 44	180	VALLEY • 47
38	CHEYENNE • 39	86	HAMILTON • 28	134	NUCKOLLS • 42	182	WASHINGTON • 29
40	CLAY • 30	88	HARLAN • 51	136	OTOE • 11	184	WAYNE • 27
42	COLFAX • 43	90	HAYES • 79	138	PAWNEE • 54	186	WEBSTER • 45
44	CUMMING • 24	92	HITCHCOCK • 67	140	PERKINS • 74	188	WHEELER • 84
46	CUSTER • 4	94	HOLT • 36	142	PHELPS • 37	190	YORK • 17
48	DAKOTA • 70	96	HOOKER • 93	144	PIERCE • 40		
50	DAWES • 69	98	HOWARD • 49	146	PLATTE • 10		
52	DAWSON • 18	100	JEFFERSON • 33	148	POLK • 41		

PREFACE

This book takes you on a journey through Nebraska's 93 county courthouses. Over the years, my wife Harriet Grossbart and I enjoyed road trips to small towns during weekends and holidays. Most often, we were drawn to the most prominent building in these communities – the county courthouse. Our weekend visits found these landmarks closed, which piqued our interest even more.

After retiring as a Lancaster County employee in 2012, I established and ultimately sold a successful business before retiring a second time in 2022.

With both Harriet and I having spent most of our careers working for county governments, we finally found ourselves with free time to explore courthouses in our adopted state on weekdays, when they were open.

A good friend frequently spoke positively about the Gosper County Courthouse in Elwood. Despite our research, we found limited information about its interior – or about the interiors of other Nebraska courthouses.

This absence of information led us to the Nebraska Association of County Officials (NACO) and then to a Lincoln architect whose portfolio included several courthouses. A passion project was born. In January 2023, Harriet and I began reaching out to county clerks and district court clerks for permission to photograph courtrooms and other interior spaces.

We conducted 82 site visits before Harriet lost her battle with cancer. I completed the remaining 11 counties with my loyal companion, Nora the Corgi, on December 7, 2023.

Over the course of 11 months and 28,000 miles, we met hundreds of people in collecting the treasure-trove of facts, lore and photographs that fill these pages.

Special thanks to my friend and neighbor Steve Graziano for suggesting the title.

And to Nebraska's county employees – all 11,000 of you. Local government is in capable hands.

Dean Settle, Author

FOREWORD

Dean Settle and I grew up under the towering presence of our respective 19th-century historic courthouses. As children, those majestic buildings were the most impressive structures we had ever encountered, their ornate designs underscoring the significance of the business conducted within their walls. With their striking towers, often embellished with bells and clocks, these courthouses have served as vital landmarks for over a century, embodying the heart of commerce in the community.

Post World War I, new courthouses abandoned the capitol style in favor of the federal style. Following World War II, the international style replaced the federal style. Regardless of these stylistic changes, the design and detailing continue to reflect a high level of integrity, preserving the sense of significance these structures embody.

In the later part of the 20th century, the international style courthouses gave way to structures with a more commercial appearance. Modern courthouses are seldom located in the commercial centers, perhaps due to our desire for convenient parking.

Throughout Nebraska's history, the exterior designs of courthouses have changed in response to taste, convenience and economics. While the exteriors of modern courthouses may be less impressive than their historic counterparts, the interiors have continued to provide integrity and a sense of importance through material selection, architectural details and art. This book provides the proof.

Jerry L. Berggren, AIA
Principal/Preservation Architect
Berggren Architects, P.C.

A common thread across the United States is the county seat, where the county courthouse stands as a central landmark. Especially in rural areas, these courthouses often become symbols of local pride, serving not only as venues for administering justice and conducting government business but also as hosts for public events and gatherings.

As both an architect and the current president of Lincoln Rotary Club 14, I am thrilled about the 2024 release of Dean Settle's passion project, "Inside Nebraska Courthouses."

From an architectural perspective, I appreciate how courthouses act as beacons for vibrant economies and communities, reflecting the unique identities and histories of the regions they serve.

As a Rotarian, I see courthouses as embodiments of Rotary's Four-Way Test, exemplifying truthfulness, fairness and a commitment to goodwill and beneficial relationships.

In the pages ahead, I'm excited for you to explore the unique character of Nebraska's courthouses and to discover the visual similarities and differences that make each one a cherished landmark in its county and our state.

Erin Dobesh, AIA
2024 President
Lincoln Rotary Club 14

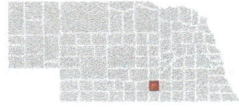

ADAMS COUNTY

COUNTY SEAT: HASTINGS • **LICENSE PLATE PREFIX: 14** • **POPULATION: 31,021**
GOVERNED BY SEVEN COUNTY SUPERVISORS

Adams County, established in 1867, was named in honor of John Adams, second president of the United States. Its first permanent settlement was made by Titus Babcock in 1871 on the present site of the town of Juniata, the original county seat. The railroad's arrival spurred growth and development, prompting the county seat's relocation to Hastings after years of tension between the two towns. To add to the drama, the county records were transported by wagon under the cover of night from Juniata to Hastings.

Today's courthouse stands in stark contrast to its predecessor, an architectural marvel constructed in 1889 using Colorado sandstone. The original's most prominent feature was a 10-foot steeple statue of the Greek goddess of justice – visible from miles around until it became unsafe and was removed in 1921. Some 40 years later, the edifice was demolished. Its replacement, built in 1962 with South Dakota marble, sits to the northeast of the site.

It was a sunny June day when we stepped inside and made a new friend in the maintenance man, who took his job seriously and eagerly offered to show us around. He led us inside vaults housing dozens of leather-bound volumes of court records from long ago and chambers where county supervisors and planning and zoning commissioners tackle issues large and small. This also is home to the Nebraska Extension and probation services. The Adams County Convention & Visitors Bureau adds a touch of hospitality.

The big surprise is on the second-floor landing where a pair of vibrant murals inject vitality into an otherwise austere stone façade. Created by art students and faculty at Hastings College, the colorful montages celebrate the community's rich history.

Shortly before noon, as the courtroom emptied, we caught a glimpse of the oak pews and swivel chairs characteristic of public buildings of the late 19th and early 20th centuries.

The courthouse was buzzing with activity as we departed and strolled down the street for lunch at What the Dickens? – a traditional British bakery, of all places!

KICKSHAWS

In the Nebraska license plate system, the prefix indicates the county's ranking based on the total number of vehicles registered in 1922, the year the system was introduced.

WHEN NEBRASKA'S COUNTIES WERE ESTABLISHED, THEY WERE TYPICALLY SIZED AT 24 MILES BY 24 MILES. PLACING THE COUNTY SEAT IN THE CENTER FACILITATED CONVENIENT HORSE-AND-BUGGY TRAVEL BEFORE THE ADVENT OF AUTOMOBILES.

ALL 93 COUNTIES BELONG TO THE NEBRASKA ASSOCIATION OF COUNTY OFFICIALS (NACO).

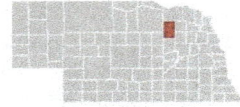

ANTELOPE COUNTY

COUNTY SEAT: NELIGH • LICENSE PLATE PREFIX: 26 • POPULATION: 6,302
GOVERNED BY FIVE COUNTY COMMISSIONERS

Antelope County, established in 1871, derives its name from the abundant pronghorn antelope that once roamed its expansive grasslands and prairie. The name was suggested by Leander Gerard, a state senator who, after killing an antelope, proposed it during the county's organizational phase.

Oakdale was the first county seat, from 1871 to 1883. The honors transferred to Neligh after fire destroyed Oakdale's frame courthouse.

The Antelope County Courthouse, one of Nebraska's oldest still in operation, blends history with modern utility. The original section, constructed between 1894 and 1895, features Romanesque Revival architecture worthy of inclusion on the National Register of Historic Places.

Today, the section serves as a hub for essential county services, including Health and Human Services, Veterans Services and a driver's license bureau open only on Wednesdays.

On the second floor, a combined district and county courtroom features a design element not seen elsewhere in Nebraska: a windowed security barrier for unruly defendants.

A flat-roofed, red brick 1960s-era annex enhances accessibility and serves as the primary public entrance.

In corridors old and new, photographs and artwork depict key moments in the history of the town and county. On the roof of the original courthouse, a golden antelope stands as a tribute to the county's namesake, serving as a timeless symbol – and a fun photo opportunity.

KICKSHAWS

Worth a visit: The Neligh Mill State Historic Site along the Elkhorn River. The 1873 mill – one of the largest of its kind in Nebraska – produced Gold Medal flour, among other popular brands, until the 1940s.

NELIGH IS THE ONLY TOWN SO NAMED IN THE UNITED STATES.

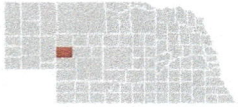

ARTHUR COUNTY

COUNTY SEAT: ARTHUR • LICENSE PLATE PREFIX: 91 • POPULATION: 485
GOVERNED BY THREE COUNTY COMMISSIONERS

While the boundaries were established in 1887, Arthur County's residents did not petition to formally organize until 1913. For those 26 years, the county came under the jurisdiction of what was then McPherson County.

The Kincaid Act of 1904 brought an influx of settlers and the platting of Arthur as the county seat nearly a decade later. The county is named in honor of the 21st president of the United States, Chester A. Arthur.

Today, Arthur County is the second-least populated in Nebraska (McPherson, from which it was carved, is the least-populated). Arthur remains its only incorporated community.

The original courthouse – cited as the smallest in the country – lacked basic amenities like running water until electricity arrived in 1925. The building still stands today and operates as a museum.

The current courthouse, a symbol of modernity upon its 1961 opening, is a hub of activity, housing the county library and serving as the village office and community meeting space.

Fifty-year employee Becky Swanson is a multitasking marvel, serving in a total of five roles – county clerk, election commissioner, assessor, register of deeds and clerk of the district court.

Court and jail services are contracted through Keith County in Ogallala, leaving the Arthur County jail primarily used for storage.

KICKSHAWS

Worth a visit:
Pilgrim Holiness Church, also known as Baled Hay Church – because it was constructed with hay bales a century ago.

In the 1920s and '30s, the Ku Klux Klan operated from a two-story building across the street from the courthouse. When the Klan failed to pay taxes, the county acquired the property and repurposed it into a community meeting space. Later, the building was sold to a local rancher and hauled to his property.

THE NEBRASKA PANHANDLE IS IN THE MOUNTAIN TIME ZONE.

BANNER COUNTY

COUNTY SEAT: HARRISBURG • LICENSE PLATE PREFIX: 85 • POPULATION: 674
GOVERNED BY THREE COUNTY COMMISSIONERS

It was a balmy December afternoon when we pulled into Harrisburg, population 59, to see its humble yet pleasant courthouse. Built in 1958, it replaces a beloved wood-frame building on the same site.

A warm reception from friendly elected officials and busy staff added to the cordial atmosphere, allowing us to freely explore. A highlight was a gallery of yesteryear photographs and maps, complemented by a vivid painting of the original courthouse.

We couldn't resist a circular metal staircase, a relic of the building's past and common to many courthouses of the 1950s and '60s, that took us to a basement storage area – and quickly back out again!

Harrisburg originally was established as Centropolis in 1886; the name change came shortly after the county's organization in 1888. Early residents were determined to become "the brightest star in the constellation of Nebraska counties," thus the county name. Although the seat of government, Harrisburg has never incorporated as a town or village.

The courthouse was marked by a daring burglary in 1964, when the clerk's vault was breached and robbed. In the east wing, the district courtroom is unassuming yet pivotal; a murder trial here in 1954 is immortalized in Robert G. Simmons Jr.'s book, "One of Our Drivers Is Missing."

The first cattle barons in western Nebraska were Edward Creighton of Omaha and his brother, John A. Creighton, who maintained large grazing herds in Banner County in the 1860s and 1870s. Edward's estate founded Omaha's Creighton University in 1878.

KICKSHAWS

The county has 22 available staff positions; five were unfilled the day we visited.

Banner County boasts the state's highest elevation. Wildcat Mountain rises a mile above sea level.

FARMING, RANCHING AND OIL DRILLING ARE THE PRIMARY ECONOMIC ACTIVITIES.

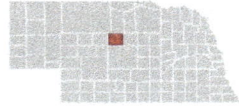

BLAINE COUNTY

COUNTY SEAT: BREWSTER • LICENSE PLATE PREFIX: 86 • POPULATION: 384
GOVERNED BY THREE COUNTY COMMISSIONERS

Built in 1908 from concrete block after its predecessor was destroyed by fire, the Blaine County Courthouse is a symbol of endurance in the heart of the Sand Hills.

The county, established in 1886, was named after James G. Blaine, the statesman from Maine who was the 1884 GOP presidential nominee.

Brewster, the county seat, is named after its founder, George W. Brewster. The homesteading newspaper publisher widely promoted the idea of locating the state capital in his fair community because of its central location. Optimistic of the prospect, he poured his fortune into constructing buildings to attract commerce. Significant population growth never resulted.

In the late 1940s, Dunning, with a population more than twice that of Brewster, made a bid for the county seat. Residents of the eastern part of the county campaigned to hold on to the seat of government, and the attempt was defeated by public vote.

In 2024, Brewster ranked as the smallest county seat in Nebraska with a population of just 12 residents, including the county clerk and the county treasurer, who are sisters. Blaine County is the third smallest county in population in the state.

The small yet formidable courthouse hosts the essentials: administrative offices, vault, courtroom, sheriff's office and meeting room. A river even runs through it. Well, more accurately, a natural spring flows under the county clerk's office – and seeps in on occasion.

The county's past is celebrated in historical maps, signs and artifacts, including a vintage fingerprint station and oddities confiscated by the sheriff's department.

KICKSHAWS

Worth a visit: For a good night's stay, try an author favorite, Uncle Buck's Lodge in Brewster.

Doc Middleton, a widely known outlaw, was a saloon keeper in Brewster in the late 1880s. He also worked at saloons in Gordon, Rushville and Valentine. He farmed with his brother, John, in Brown County and had ranches in Rock and Sheridan Counties.

IN NEBRASKA, 65 PERCENT OF COUNTIES USE THE COMMISSION FORM OF COUNTY GOVERNMENT, WHILE 35 PERCENT UTILIZE A BOARD OF SUPERVISORS SYSTEM.

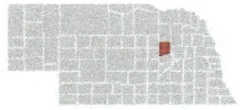

BOONE COUNTY

COUNTY SEAT: ALBION • LICENSE PLATE PREFIX: 23 • POPULATION: 5,310
GOVERNED BY THREE COUNTY COMMISSIONERS

In 1871, the land that would become Boone County was a rich hunting and trapping ground for the Pawnee and Sioux Tribes. Just a month after the Nebraska Legislature established and organized the county, naming it in honor of the Kentucky frontiersman Daniel Boone, the first white settlers arrived and began constructing sod houses along Beaver Creek.

The selection of the county seat was a contentious affair between Albion and Boone, the only two towns with post offices at the time. Albion ultimately emerged victorious in the 1874 election, though not without a fight. Six years later, Albion saw its first trains roll in, marking a new chapter in its development.

The current courthouse is the county's third iteration, inaugurated in 1976. A notable feature is the preservation of the original 1897 courthouse's brick tower clock as a freestanding element near the main entrance.

The single-level brick building is both spacious and immaculate. Its corridors hold inspirational sayings, maps, original artwork and old-time ranching photos. Don't miss the vintage license plate display in the treasurer's office. Or the Nebraska-shaped puzzle with interlocking pieces.

The courtroom is handsome, featuring well-maintained minimalist 1990s office furniture. During our visit, courthouse staff eagerly anticipated Government Day, a program designed to educate local high school students about civic engagement and governance.

KICKSHAWS

Albion's name was selected through euchre, a game of chance. Two men played for Albion; two for the name of Manchester.

Several Nebraska counties have had as many as four county seat locations.

Settlers along the Cedar River in the southwestern corner of the county in 1879 initially named their community "Cedar Falls." It soon changed to "Cedar Rapids" because there were no falls – only rapids – on that stretch of the river.

ALL NEBRASKA COURTHOUSES ARE CLOSED ON ARBOR DAY,
AN OBSERVANCE FOUNDED BY J. STERLING MORTON IN NEBRASKA CITY ON APRIL 10, 1872,
DEDICATED TO TREE PLANTING AND CONSERVATION.

BOX BUTTE COUNTY

COUNTY SEAT: ALLIANCE • LICENSE PLATE PREFIX: 65 • POPULATION: 10,692
GOVERNED BY THREE COUNTY COMMISSIONERS

Box Butte County takes its name from a flat-topped hill northwest of Alliance that served as a landmark for miners and freighters headed to the Black Hills during the gold rush of the 1870s.

In 1886, when the county was established, the wife of homesteader W.A. Bissell suggested that "Box Butte" would be a more lasting and appropriate name for the county than that of "some man who had climbed to fame."

Hemingford was initially settled by Canadian immigrants in the summer of 1885. It secured the county seat from rival Nonpariel in 1890 but lost it to Alliance in a heated contest in 1899, a shift largely driven by the railroad. The courthouse, in fact, was relocated 20 miles on railroad flatbed cars from Hemingford to Alliance.

The town's Beaux-Arts courthouse was built in 1913. The interior boasts walls of white marble with delicate gray veining, while the floors are adorned with white hexagonal tiles bordered with a terracotta chainlike pattern.

The focal point of the first level is the state seal, an intricate tile inlay. Overhead, a stained-glass dome refracts light under a clear blue sky. Stepping deeper into the interior, globe light fixtures, cast-iron staircases and classical columns from the early 20th century add to the grandeur of the corridors.

The courtrooms are impressive, with handsome wood trim. An extensive law library houses vaults carefully organized and equipped with fireproof metal window shades. On the third floor, the old jail has been repurposed for storage since a law enforcement complex, including a modern jail, was built in 1978. Today, the sheriff's office and the Alliance Police Department share space in this thriving county hub. Nebraska Extension maintains an office here as well, actively supporting 4-H programs in the county.

KICKSHAWS

The county is the home of Carhenge, Nebraska's quirky version of England's Stonehenge, made from old cars painted gray.

Box Butte County only has two towns, Alliance and Hemingford, and one unincorporated town, Berea.

The Alliance Municipal Airport and the Nebraska Veterans Cemetery occupy a former major military training field.

ALLIANCE SITS AT THE JUNCTION OF NEBRASKA HIGHWAY 2 – THE SAND HILLS JOURNEY SCENIC BYWAY – AND U.S HIGHWAY 385, THE GOLD RUSH BYWAY.

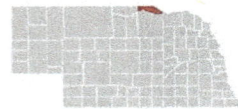

BOYD COUNTY

COUNTY SEAT: BUTTE • LICENSE PLATE PREFIX: 63 • POPULATION: 1,725
GOVERNED BY SEVEN COUNTY SUPERVISORS

Originally Native American land, Boyd County was officially organized in 1891 and is situated between the South Dakota state line, the Missouri River and the Niobrara River.

The county was named in honor of James E. Boyd, the one-time mayor of Omaha who was governor of Nebraska at the time the county was organized.

Butte, the county seat, derives its name from the rocky elevations south of town, thought to have been created from deposits by icebergs that carved rivers thousands of years ago.

A portion of the county was part of the Fort Randall military reservation from 1856 to 1892.

The present courthouse, a contemporary structure from 1966, features offices along a main hall. The walls are adorned with community photographs, including ones of the original courthouse, a wooden rendering of the county flag and a large map of the 545-square-mile county.

The basement serves as storage for various items, among them old ballot boxes. Vaults in the offices of the clerk and treasurer safeguard the county's plats and documents, including early property lists.

The grounds feature the old jail, which, while no longer in use, remains a captivating site. Notably, decades ago, a cattle thief was lynched here.

KICKSHAWS

The controversial Keystone XL pipeline, first proposed in the early 2010s, would have passed through parts of Boyd County as well as other areas in Nebraska. The pipeline was intended to transport crude oil from Canada to the Gulf Coast but faced significant environmental and legal challenges. It became a focal point of debate regarding energy policy, environmental impact and land rights in Nebraska and beyond.

Boyd County was the site of a controversial failed attempt in the late 1980s to establish a nuclear waste facility a few miles west of the courthouse.

SCENIC NEBRASKA HIGHWAY 12 CROSSES THE COUNTY FROM EAST TO WEST.

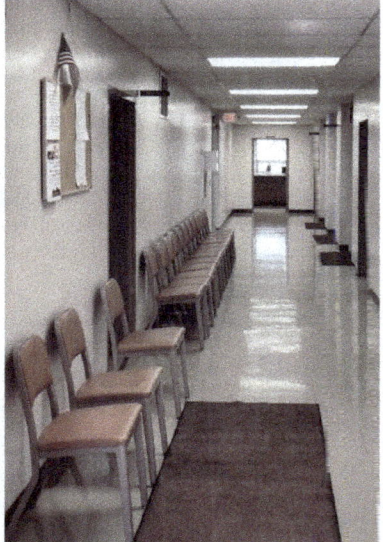

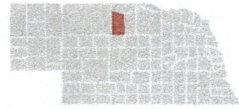

BROWN COUNTY

COUNTY SEAT: AINSWORTH • LICENSE PLATE PREFIX: 75 • POPULATION: 2,853
GOVERNED BY THREE COUNTY COMMISSIONERS

In the mid-19th century, governance in this region was managed solely from military posts. In 1876, Holt County was officially organized, with Brown County attached to it. When Brown County finally was established in 1883, the legislative bill proposing its creation notably lacked a specified sponsor.

At that time, five members of the legislature shared the surname Brown, and in keeping with the conventions of the period, none used their first names on official documents. Although some accounts attribute the naming to Charles H. Brown, a senator from Omaha, the exact origin of the name remains unclear.

We do know, however, that the county seat was named for James Ainsworth, the civil engineer in charge of the rail work there.

The original courthouse, built in 1888, was destroyed by fire on Easter in 1958. County offices were housed in buildings on main street for almost four years while a replacement was built.

Today, the two-level, fireproof structure is well maintained and includes a wing specifically for the district court.

On the upper level, walls leading to elected officials' offices hold quilts, maps and the Brown County flag. The austere lower level, with chair glide access, accommodates the county court, Nebraska Extension, a meeting room and an area for administering driver's license exams.

The district court wing has a midcentury modern aesthetic, complete with a collection of photos celebrating past judges. Adjacent to the courtroom are offices for court staff, a jury room and a law library.

KICKSHAWS

Worth a look in the area:
The 56,000-acre Niobrara Valley Preserve, one of the largest Nature Conservancy sites in the nation.

Forty-three percent of Brown County's residents are of German heritage.

HISTORICALLY, 20 PERCENT OF NEBRASKA COURTHOUSES HAVE BEEN DESTROYED BY FIRE.

BUFFALO COUNTY

COUNTY SEAT: KEARNEY • LICENSE PLATE PREFIX: 9 • POPULATION: 50,697
GOVERNED BY SEVEN COUNTY COMMISSIONERS

Kearney's sesquicentennial (150th) celebration was the perfect occasion to visit the Buffalo County Courthouse. In operation since 1974, this modern, single-level building replaced a grand structure that, despite surviving a major fire in 1935, had outlived its usefulness.

The courthouse features buffalo taxidermy and sculptures, and near the entrance, two striking murals – one of a covered wagon and one of a bison – in tribute to the county's early history.

Established in 1855 and named for the vast herds of bison that once roamed the region, the county's development was shaped by both the Mormon Trail and the Union Pacific Railroad.

Originally in nearby Gibbon, the county seat was quietly shifted to Kearney in 1874, ostensibly to prevent disputes as Kearney grew rapidly because of the railroad's arrival.

During that time, Moses H. Sydenham, a Buffalo County pioneer, founded a newspaper in Kearney and used it to promote his idea of centralized Kearney as the capital of the United States.

KICKSHAWS

In the late 19th and early 20th centuries, the location of county seats in many regions of the United States was often influenced significantly by the advent of cross-country railroads.

The Nebraska Association of County Officials (NACO) was founded in 1894. Its 130th anniversary celebration, scheduled for December 2024 in Kearney, coincided with the release of this book.

Buffalo County is one of only two counties in Nebraska named for an animal. The other is Antelope County.

BUFFALO COUNTY IS ONE OF THE LARGEST COUNTIES IN THE STATE WITH 975 SQUARE MILES.

BURT COUNTY

COUNTY SEAT: TEKAMAH • LICENSE PLATE PREFIX: 31 • POPULATION: 6,727
GOVERNED BY SEVEN COUNTY SUPERVISORS

Burt County was established in 1854, a half-century after Lewis and Clark passed through the area and three years before the first recorded settlers put down roots at present-day Oakland.

Prior to white settlement, the area was the domain of the Omaha and Ponca Tribes.

The county was named in honor of Francis Burt of South Carolina, Nebraska's first territorial governor. He died October 18, 1854, two days after taking office.

Tekamah, the count seat, was incorporated in 1855 and went without a courthouse for 23 years. In 1917, the cornerstone for its four-story Beaux-Arts marvel was laid by the local Grand Lodge of Masons – a common practice in the 19th and early 20th centuries across the United States.

This development marked a significant milestone for the community, which had previously conducted county business from various downtown buildings over the preceding two decades.

The formality of Beaux-Arts style is particularly seen in the woodwork and tile throughout the building, including the offices of elected officials and the entryway, where the Nebraska State Seal is rendered in inlaid terrazzo tile.

A marble staircase leads to second-floor offices and an ambitious patriotic mural by local artist Deanna Johnson. This striking artwork flows around walls, windows and doors, creating a moving tribute to veterans from the Civil War to present day.

Historical photos and maps enhance the visual narrative of the county's evolution. Radiators on each floor are reminders of the building's age, while obsolete jail cells on the top floor now store files and documents, with a whimsical mannequin playfully posing as a "prisoner."

KICKSHAWS

Nebraska's original eight counties were Burt, Cass, Dodge, Douglas, Forney, Pierce, Richardson and Washington.

Courthouses in the 19th century were the largest buildings in the county, providing meeting space for lodges, churches, social, civic and veterans groups. And public restrooms.

BUTLER COUNTY

COUNTY SEAT: DAVID CITY • LICENSE PLATE PREFIX: 25 • POPULATION: 8,459
GOVERNED BY SEVEN COUNTY SUPERVISORS

Butler County's history began in 1856, when it was named in honor of William Orlando Butler of Kentucky, who had turned down an appointment to be Nebraska's first territorial governor.

The county's first significant settlement was established in 1857 near the present site of Linwood. Originally, Savannah served as the county seat, but it was moved to David City after four elections.

Butler County's gently rolling hills became known as the Bohemian Alps, thanks to the Czech immigrants from Bohemia and Moravia who migrated to the region in the last decades of the 19th century.

The current courthouse, constructed in 1964-65, marks a notable shift from its late 19th-century Richardsonian Romanesque predecessor with bell tower. Spanning an entire city block, the single-story design emphasizes efficiency, a hallmark of midcentury civic architecture.

During our rainy-day visit, the courthouse was bustling with activity, helped by an integrated sheriff's office, jail and juvenile center.

Another highlight: modern fireproof vaults for county documents – a feature not all counties are equipped with for record preservation.

Nebraska's courthouses not only are centers of justice but also places of community remembrance and appreciation for those who have served our country. We enjoyed Butler County's tributes on the courthouse grounds.

KICKSHAWS

The hills of Butler County were originally the homeland of the Pawnee Tribe.

Nebraska counties built 67 courthouses with towers from 1882 to 1909.

 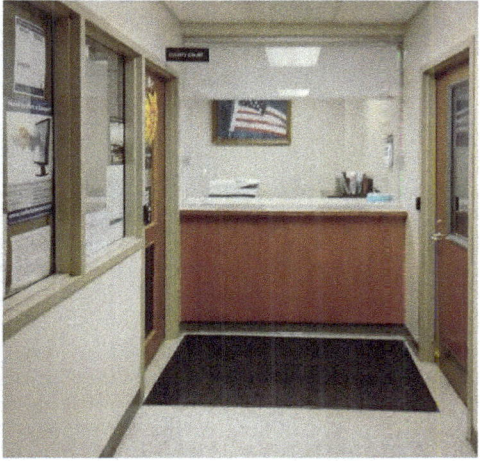

SINCE WORLD WAR II, COURTHOUSE VAULTS HAVE DOUBLED AS WORKSPACES FOR ELECTED OFFICIALS.

CASS COUNTY

COUNTY SEAT: PLATTSMOUTH • LICENSE PLATE PREFIX: 20 • POPULATION: 27,446
GOVERNED BY FIVE COUNTY COMMISSIONERS

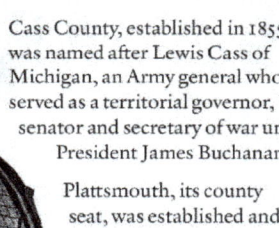

Cass County, established in 1855, was named after Lewis Cass of Michigan, an Army general who served as a territorial governor, U.S. senator and secretary of war under President James Buchanan.

Plattsmouth, its county seat, was established and mapped a year earlier as the Plattsmouth Town Company. The town was approved in 1855 by the Nebraska Territorial Legislature and named for its geographic proximity to the Platte and Missouri Rivers. Significant settlement, however, didn't come until 1858, when the town won the designation of county seat.

The current courthouse – the county's third – was built in 1891 and listed on the National Register of Historic Places in 1990. Designed by architect William Gray of Lincoln (also known for his work in Hamilton and Johnson Counties), it's constructed in terra-cotta, brick and Wisconsin brownstone.

Originally featuring 24 fireplaces, the courthouse now boasts 34 heat pumps. Noteworthy interior elements include lofty ceilings, tall windows and doors, decorative tiled floors and distinctive wooden newel posts. The district courtroom stands out for its ornate wood carvings behind the judge's bench and in the jury box, as well as Victorian-era door hardware and wainscoting.

A key attraction for visitors of all ages is the clock and bell tower, accessible via stairs where walls have been signed by people who have made the trek. At the summit, you're rewarded with a panoramic view of the confluence of the Platte and Missouri Rivers.

In 2002, the City County Law Enforcement Center was constructed adjacent to the courthouse to hold the sheriff's office, Plattsmouth Police Department and a 100-cell jail.

KICKSHAWS

Each commissioner represents a different township within the county.

In the USA, there are 3,144 county courthouses. Texas leads with 254, one in each county. Currently, 36 U.S. counties have dual county seats.

One of the largest Indian battles on the western frontier occurred between the Omaha and Otoe Tribes along Weeping Water Creek.

FRENCH EXPLORERS WERE IN THE AREA IN THE 1730s.

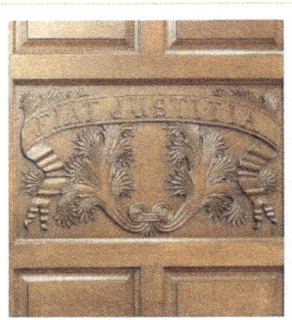

CEDAR COUNTY

COUNTY SEAT: HARTINGTON • LICENSE PLATE PREFIX: 13 • POPULATION: 8,262
GOVERNED BY THREE COUNTY SUPERVISORS

The Lewis and Clark Expedition passed through what became Cedar County in 1804. The county was officially established in 1857 and named for the abundant cedar trees in the region. The county seat moved twice before finally settling in Hartington.

In 1891, the community commissioned J.C. Stitt of Norfolk to design a courthouse in the robust Romanesque style of the era.

A century later, in 2009, an addition was integrated into the original courthouse, giving administrative offices, vaults, and historic maps, photographs and artifacts a new home.

In the original courthouse section, there's a quiet law library on the lower level, while the ground floor bustles with activities of the county attorney, county court and probation offices.

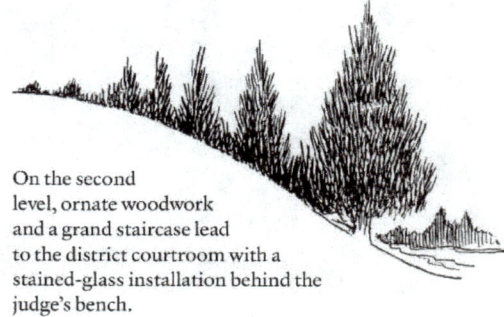

On the second level, ornate woodwork and a grand staircase lead to the district courtroom with a stained-glass installation behind the judge's bench.

On the Friday afternoon of my visit, the courtroom buzzed with festivity. A reception was underway to honor the inauguration of a new county judge, drawing together community members, legal professionals, local officials and family members.

KICKSHAWS

After World War I, Nebraska courthouses stopped being built with towers for economic and practical reasons.

Three British notables were visiting the United States as towns were being named in Cedar County: politician and nobleman Lord Hartington; orator Lord Randolph Churchill (father of Winston); and judge and politician Lord John Duke Coleridge (grandson of poet Samuel Taylor Coleridge). The younger Coleridge actually visited the town site named for him.

The history of the area can be traced to the 1650s, when the Omaha, Ponca and Sioux Tribes all had encampments here.

THE CEDAR COUNTY COURTHOUSE
IS A SUCCESSFUL BLENDING OF OLD AND NEW.

CHASE COUNTY

COUNTY SEAT: IMPERIAL • LICENSE PLATE PREFIX: 72 • POPULATION: 3,724
GOVERNED BY THREE COUNTY COMMISSIONERS

Chase County served as a vital watering stop for cattle drives along the Great Western Trail, which ended at Ogallala, the Union Pacific railhead.

The county's boundaries were established by the legislature in 1873, but the organization of the county did not begin until 1886. At the time, Chase was part of Hayes County and populated 100 percent by cowboys and ranch families.

The county was named for Champion S. Chase, the first attorney general of Nebraska in 1867. Prior to that, Chase had been mayor of Omaha.

Built in 1911 to replace a predecessor destroyed by fire after only a year, the courthouse impresses with timeless elegance. Its visual appeal includes marble tile floors, innovative light-filtering glass block and original 19th-century features such as a clerk's counter and a cast-iron spiral staircase.

Throughout the courthouse, prints, etchings and maps tell the county's story. The most unexpected discovery? A cribbage board shaped like Nebraska! For years, the building served as the social center of the community, hosting worship services, school programs and dances.

Congratulations to the dedicated stewards of this important landmark. The daily operation and upkeep of such a treasure takes work.

KICKSHAWS

North of Wauneta lies an area with significant loess deposits, characterized by steep-walled canyons.

The Apache Tribe had an earth-lodge settlement in Chase County between 1675 and 1725.

Chase County has six listings on the National Register of Historic Places, including the courthouse and two flour mills.

THE COURTHOUSE IN IMPERIAL IS A SYMBOL OF COMMUNITY RESOLVE, HAVING SECURED ITS STATUS AS THE COUNTY SEAT THROUGH THREE CONTENTIOUS ELECTIONS.

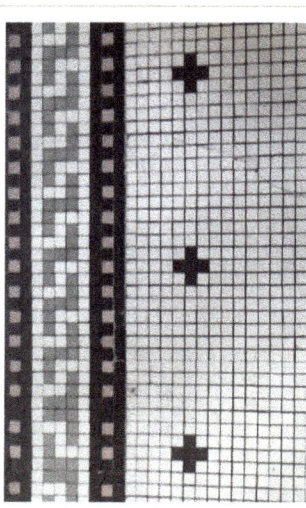  

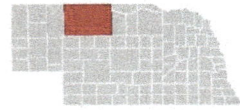

CHERRY COUNTY

COUNTY SEAT: VALENTINE · LICENSE PLATE PREFIX: 66 · POPULATION: 5,492
GOVERNED BY THREE COUNTY COMMISSIONERS

Cherry County, established in 1883, was named in honor of Lt. Samuel A. Cherry of the 5th U.S. Cavalry. He was slain on May 11, 1881, near Fort Niobrara.

The county seat was named for Edward K. Valentine, a U.S. congressman from Nebraska and sergeant-at-arms of the U.S. Senate.

The original courthouse was built in 1901; an annex was added in 1954 to accommodate offices for the county roads department and larger courtrooms. The Cherry County Sheriff is co-located with the Valentine Police Department.

In 2011, plans were underway for a major renovation of the courthouse. At the same time, the county acquired the old post office across the street, which is notable for its mural by American artist Kady Faulkner (1901-1977). Entitled "End of the Line," this 1939 artwork was commissioned by the Works Progress Administration (WPA) during President Franklin D. Roosevelt's New Deal program.

Time was well spent exploring the prints and etchings and a captivating marble sculpture within the courthouse. Additionally, the county flag proudly bearing the phrase "God's Own Cow Country" brought a smile.

For more on Cherry County, read "A Sandhill Century" by Marianne Brinda.

KICKSHAWS

Cherry County is America's top beef cow county with 184,716 cows, more than twice the number as the county with the second most, Holt County, according to a 2024 Drovers Report.

DeWitty (ultimately renamed Audacious) in Cherry County was the most successful settlement of Black homesteaders in Nebraska under the Kincaid Act of the late 19th and early 20th centuries. Today all that remains is a Nebraska Historic Site marker.

CHERRY COUNTY IS THE LARGEST IN THE NATION BY AREA, SPANNING 5,961 SQUARE MILES – ABOUT THE SIZE OF CONNECTICUT. IT HAS 1,100 MILES OF ROADS AND 88 BRIDGES.

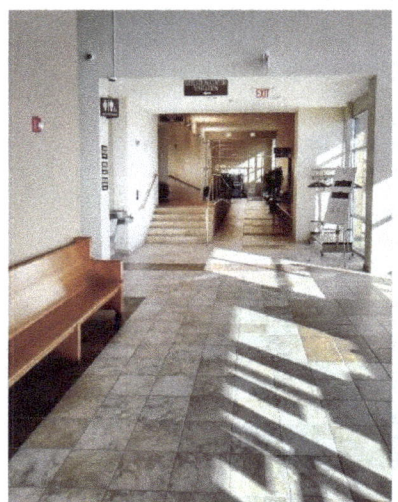  

CHEYENNE COUNTY

COUNTY SEAT: SIDNEY · LICENSE PLATE PREFIX: 39 · POPULATION: 9,541
GOVERNED BY THREE COUNTY COMMISSIONERS

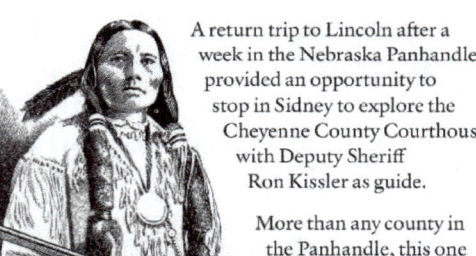

A return trip to Lincoln after a week in the Nebraska Panhandle provided an opportunity to stop in Sidney to explore the Cheyenne County Courthouse with Deputy Sheriff Ron Kissler as guide.

More than any county in the Panhandle, this one experienced rapid development. Established in 1871, it was named after the Cheyenne Indians who first inhabited the region. Sidney quickly began drawing a diverse array of settlers, merchants, freighters, cowboys, soldiers, railroaders, wheat farmers and cattle ranchers.

By the 1880s, the town was thriving as a military post, a railhead for Texas cattle shipments and a major distribution center for freighting operations to the Black Hills gold mines in Dakota Territory.

The Cheyenne County courthouse, constructed between 1966 and 1967, is the fourth iteration on the site. Its predecessor, dating to 1911, was razed in 1968.

The tidy and spacious interior features glazed brick main walls and midcentury mod mosaic tile. Courtrooms boast midcentury style with walnut finishes. The treasurer's office includes a bulletin board adorned with vintage license plates, a sure-fire conversation-starter. The vault holds bound volumes of county records, securely stored yet readily accessible – convenient when doing research.

More than a legal center, the courthouse is a hub for essential services, including the sheriff's office, county jail and Health and Human Services.

KICKSHAWS

In 1942, the Sioux Army Depot was established near Sidney to support the logistical needs of the U.S. military during World War II.

Oil was discovered here in 1949.

Outdoor sporting goods retailer Cabela's was founded in Sidney in 1961 as a mail-order company specializing in fishing and hunting gear, with thousands of employees. Bass Pro Shops bought Cabela's in 2017, closing the Sidney headquarters.

IN THE MID-1800s, SIDNEY, WITH ITS MIX OF PIONEERS, WAS KNOWN AS THE WICKEDEST TOWN IN THE WEST.

CLAY COUNTY

COUNTY SEAT: CLAY CENTER • LICENSE PLATE PREFIX: 30 • POPULATION: 6,116
GOVERNED BY SEVEN COUNTY SUPERVISORS

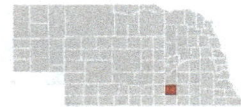

The Clay County Courthouse, which opened in 1921, emerged from a contentious battle with Sutton for the county seat.

Despite ongoing banter about the seat being "stolen," the courthouse remains a source of pride for the entire county.

Clay County was established in 1855 and named after Kentucky statesman Henry Clay. By 1890, the county had a population of more than 16,000 residents.

The county, in the heart of the Rainwater Basin in south-central Nebraska, has 16 state and national waterfowl and wildlife management areas. It's known for the spectacle of migrating geese and other waterfowl each spring and fall.

The county's meticulously maintained courthouse, designed by William F. Gernandt in Nebraska, is a superb example of Beaux-Arts architecture and is listed on the National Register of Historic Places. Gernandt had a total of 10 courthouses in Nebraska and another 10 across the Midwest to his credit.

Each floor of the Clay County Courthouse features dramatic and distinctive tile work, marble stairs, newels and wainscoting, and original doors and light fixtures.

The treasurer's collection of license tags and a memorial to an early sheriff who died in the line of duty are focal points in the halls. Alongside maps, prints and local artwork, the county flag and a 50th anniversary Vietnam War flag are prominently displayed.

The old jail now serves as storage while the county court conducts its proceedings in more modern and respectable surroundings. The standout attraction is the recently renovated district courtroom, showcasing beautiful woodwork, a detailed ceiling and updated lighting.

The re-do added an impressive well-appointed jury box and spacious jury room as well.

KICKSHAWS

Pioneers from Sweden, Germany and Russia settled the area.

Many Nebraska counties are situated above the High Plains Aquifer, also known as the Ogallala Aquifer.

COLFAX COUNTY

COUNTY SEAT: SCHUYLER • LICENSE PLATE PREFIX: 43 • POPULATION: 10,566
GOVERNED BY THREE COUNTY COMMISSIONERS

Colfax County was named after Schuyler Colfax, who served as vice president of the United States under President Ulysses S. Grant. The county was established in 1869, two years after Nebraska achieved statehood. The period marked a significant chapter in the expansion and development of counties across the western United States.

The current courthouse, constructed between 1921 and 1922, replaced an earlier building that had apartments for county officers and jail cells for prisoners. Lincoln architect George Berlinghof's design features impressive marble floors and stairs and several original light fixtures.

On the first floor, you'll find a community room, Veterans Services and a driver's licensing exam office. Elected officials are located on the second floor, while the county and district courts operate on the third floor. The sheriff's office is on the fourth floor. Across the street, an annex houses the county attorney's office.

Walls throughout these spaces display photos, maps and signage in both English and Spanish while the grounds feature numerous veteran memorials.

In the 1880s, three lynchings and two murders were recorded in Colfax County. In one of the lynchings, the coroner's jury brought in a verdict of "death by hanging at the hands of parties unknown."

Between 1857 and 1919, Nebraska recorded 57 lynchings, the last of which occurred in Omaha. Among the victims, two were women, five were white, while the majority were Black. The racially motivated lynchings often took place near courthouses and jails, with mobs executing 42 people – 21 more than the state itself had executed. Some victims were already sentenced to death, but mob impatience led to bypassing legal processes.

KICKSHAWS

To establish the county, the organizing settlers and local officials had to take on half of the original county's debt.

The original courthouse once featured large trees from which two or three horse thieves were reportedly hung.

In May 2020, Colfax County had the sixth highest per capita COVID-19 infection rate of any U.S. county.

MANY 19TH-CENTURY COURTHOUSES INCLUDED HOUSING FOR SHERIFFS AND ACCOMMODATIONS FOR TRAVELING JUDGES AND COUNTY OFFICIALS.

CUMING COUNTY

COUNTY SEAT: WEST POINT • LICENSE PLATE PREFIX: 24 • POPULATION: 8,918
GOVERNED BY SEVEN COUNTY SUPERVISORS

The district courtroom of the Cuming County Courthouse features Nebraska's largest mural, painted by Frank J. Zimmerer in 1955 for the 100th anniversary of the county. Born in Nebraska City, Zimmerer also produced a mural for the Otoe County Courthouse.

West Point got its name as early as about 1858 because it was the farthest outpost or "point" west along the Elkhorn River Valley. Thomas B. Cuming, for whom the county was named, was the first secretary and acting governor of the Nebraska Territory.

The current courthouse, designed by B.H. Backlund of Omaha and built in 1954, embraces the Prairie style.

The formal entrance on the west side is now less used, with the east entrance near street parking serving as the preferred access point, equipped with an elevator.

The basement houses an active Veterans Services office and a collection of prints and displays. It also serves as a hub for driver's license exams. The main level accommodates county offices. The day of our visit, county officials were preparing for Government Day for local high school juniors.

The board of supervisors convenes in a conference room adjacent to the clerk's office. Modern stairs lead to the next level, where courtrooms are appointed with midcentury wood paneling. There also is an extensive law library and a gallery of authentic Wanted Posters. The top floor of the courthouse is dedicated to the sheriff's office and the county's emergency dispatch center.

KICKSHAWS

DeWitt was the first permanent settlement in Cuming County, with a post office established in 1858. The same year, it challenged West Point for the county seat designation. Today, all that remains of DeWitt is a sod home and a cemetery.

County clerks keep county school attendance archives, often used by genealogists.

IN THE CUMING COUNTY COURTHOUSE'S MURAL, PIONEERS ARE SHOWN ARRIVING IN THE REGION. TIME HAS TAKEN ITS TOLL ON THE RENDERING, HOWEVER, LEAVING IT IN NEED OF RESTORATION.

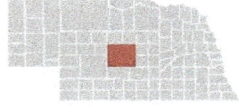

CUSTER COUNTY

COUNTY SEAT: BROKEN BOW • LICENSE PLATE PREFIX: 4 • POPULATION: 10,581
GOVERNED BY SEVEN COUNTY SUPERVISORS

Constructed in 1912, the Custer County Courthouse replaced its predecessor, which was lost to fire. Designed in the Neoclassical style by Omaha architect John Latenser, it incorporates elements that enhance its fire resistance.

Beautiful tile floors lead to county offices adorned with flags, yesteryear photos, maps and narratives on the county's namesake, Gen. George Armstrong Custer. The Civil War veteran died on the Plains, leading his cavalry regiment at the Battle of the Little Big Horn.

When the county was organized in 1877, Milo F. Young's log ranch house served as the temporary county seat. Seven years later, the county records were moved to Callaway.

In 1882, Broken Bow won the designation of county seat, and Jess Gandy donated the sites for both the county courthouse and the city square.

The interior of today's courthouse features original 19th-century furniture, a period clock, a mural and a display case with an old postal scale and early seals. The staircase boasts rare twin iron newel posts, while original doors and hardware contribute to the building's historical authenticity. The courtroom itself is handsome, reflecting the dignified architecture of its era.

In February 2017, the county consolidated its law enforcement and court facilities to the Judicial Center, a seven-acre campus one mile west of downtown Broken Bow. The move successfully enhanced community development and provided a modern setting for judicial services while preserving the historic courthouse for administrative functions and public engagement.

KICKSHAWS

In the 1880s, two men were fatally shot in Custer County for starting a prairie fire.

"Courthouses are the center of their communities. They represent art and culture and, yes, they are where you pay your taxes."
— *Allen J. Beermann, former secretary of state of Nebraska*

DAKOTA COUNTY

COUNTY SEAT: DAKOTA CITY • LICENSE PLATE PREFIX: 70 • POPULATION: 21,268
GOVERNED BY FIVE COUNTY COMMISSIONERS

Dakota County's establishment was the first act of the newly formed Nebraska Territorial Legislature on March 7, 1855.

It came on the heels of a treaty with the Omaha Indians that opened land west of the Missouri River to settlement and relocated the tribe to its present-day Thurston County reservation.

The county, named for the Dakota Indians in Sioux Nation, didn't assume its present boundaries until 1889. The word "Dakota," from the Dakota and Sioux Tribes, means "ally" or 'brother."

Today's courthouse anchors a sprawling campus currently undergoing enhancements, including upgrades to the jail facilities. Built between 1940 and 1941, the L-shaped courthouse exemplifies the straightforward and utilitarian design typical of WPA-funded structures. Its cream-colored stucco and concrete exterior lend it a look more reminiscent of a hospital or school than a traditional courthouse.

Inside, the hallways feature maps, the county flag and selected artworks, all framed by the motto, "In God We Trust."

In the district courtroom, photographs of former judges underscore the courthouse's role in preserving local judicial history.

Throughout the state, courthouse staff are generally eager to offer a tour. The hospitality shown by the county clerk and the district court clerk was especially appreciated, even as citizens lined up for vehicle license plate renewals and applications.

KICKSHAWS

Dakota County is part of the Sioux City Metropolitan Statistical Area encompassing parts of Iowa, Nebraska and South Dakota.

IN THE 1930s AND 1940s, WPA ASSISTANCE AIDED IN BUILDING NINE NEBRASKA COURTHOUSES.

DAWES COUNTY

COUNTY SEAT: CHADRON • LICENSE PLATE PREFIX: 69 • POPULATION: 8,133
GOVERNED BY THREE COUNTY COMMISSIONERS

John Latenser & Sons of Omaha was the architect on the Art Deco-style Dawes County Courthouse, constructed in 1936-1937. County funds were supplemented with contributions from the WPA after the first courthouse was destroyed by fire.

The county itself was established in 1885, carved out of Sioux County and named after James William Dawes, governor of Nebraska from 1883 to 1887. The area has a rich history influenced by the Oglala and Brule Tribes and fur traders.

The courthouse's T-shaped floorplan features a striking lobby with patterned terrazzo flooring and an antique globe light fixture. Additional period details, including woodwork, doors, stairs, newel posts and ironwork, contributed to the courthouse's inclusion on the National Register of Historic Places.

The lower level houses the probation office and the DMV. On the second floor, you'll find the courtrooms, jury room and sheriff's office. The district courtroom is particularly attractive, featuring a curved bar and photographs of judges past and present. The third floor is dedicated to the jail.

KICKSHAWS

Former Nebraska State Sen. Sandy Scofield's great-grandfather, R.E. Hinkle, had a heart attack and died on the front steps of the courthouse. He was Dawes County attorney at the time.

THE SAND HILLS REGION SPANS 20 NEBRASKA COUNTIES.

 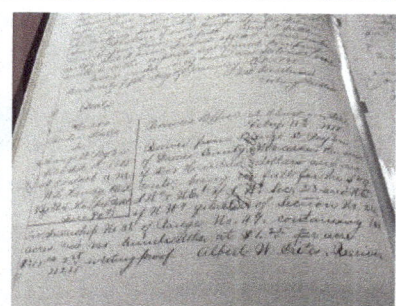 

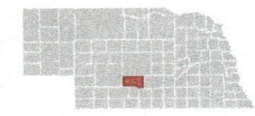

DAWSON COUNTY

COUNTY SEAT: LEXINGTON • LICENSE PLATE PREFIX: 18 • POPULATION: 24,085
GOVERNED BY FIVE COUNTY COMMISSIONERS

Dawson County, established in 1860 and formally organized in 1871, was long believed to be named after Jacob Dawson, the first postmaster of Lancaster (now Lincoln). A newspaper article from 1860 suggests that the honor actually goes to John L. Dawson, a Pennsylvania congressman and territorial governor of Kansas under President Franklin Pierce.

The current Beaux-Arts courthouse, designed by William F. Gernandt, rose in 1912-1914, replacing a wooden structure.

Dawson County takes pride in its bilingualism and boasts excellent signage throughout both the original building and 1955 office building. The terrazzo floors and black iron stairs and railings contrast beautifully with the smooth Georgia marble.

The first floor accommodates elected officials, the surveyor, road department and the driver's licensing exam area.

The second floor houses the county court, county attorney, probation, Court Appointed Special Advocates (CASA), victim witness unit, child support enforcement and jail visitation areas.

On the third floor, there's the district court and the clerk of the district court's office. The courtroom, with an adjacent jury room, is furnished with a honey oak judge's bench and jury box.

A recent visit saw the retirement of District Court Judge James E. Doyle IV, who was winding down his service after more than two decades on the bench.

KICKSHAWS

Historically, a Nebraska county could organize when its population reached 200.

Spotted at the Dawson County History Museum:
"Men do not learn very much from the lessons of history is the most important of all the lessons of history."
– *Aldous Huxley*

ADDITIONAL REMODELING PROJECTS ARE BEING DISCUSSED AS DAWSON COUNTY CONTINUES TO GROW.

DEUEL COUNTY

COUNTY SEAT: CHAPPELL • LICENSE PLATE PREFIX: 78 • POPULATION: 1,871
GOVERNED BY THREE COUNTY COMMISSIONERS

In 1888, when Cheyenne County was subdivided into five new counties, Deuel County emerged as one of them. However, in 1910, Deuel was divided to create Garden County, which reduced Deuel to the smallest county in the Panhandle. Named in honor of Harry Porter Deuel, a pioneer railroad official from Omaha, the county initially planned to have its courthouse located in Big Springs. This decision was met with resistance from the towns of Froid and Chappell, who insisted on a vote.

In January 1889, Chappell was designated as the temporary county seat in an initial election. The following month, a run-off election among the three towns led to Froid filing a court injunction against its rivals, accusing them of ballot stuffing. It took two years of legal battles before Chappell was officially confirmed as the county seat.

The current courthouse, in the Classical Revival style, was completed in 1915. The three-story structure features the original oak staircase, along with several time-worn but still functional counters and cabinets.

The lower level houses the sheriff's office, while the first floor accommodates the offices of elected officials, the county board meeting room, DMV services and the clerk of the district court. The halls are adorned with photos, the county flag, county maps and a plaque commemorating the now-decommissioned USS Deuel, a WWII amphibious attack transport. A painting of U.S. Congresswoman Virginia Smith hangs on the main floor; her longtime residence is just east of the courthouse.

On the upper level are the courtroom, law library and offices for probation, the county attorney and the road department. The heavily paneled courtroom is modestly furnished with pedestal swivel chairs for jurors and banquet-style chairs for the gallery.

KICKSHAWS

County seat elections were always competitive. Official counts typically were higher than the total number of people and animals in the county. The outcomes often were the same as if no extreme methods had been taken.

Virginia Smith served Nebraska's 3rd Congressional District from 1975 to 1991. She also was president of the American Farm Bureau Women. Her home is next door to the courthouse.

INTERSTATE 80 AND U.S. HIGHWAY 30 IN NEBRASKA GENERALLY RETRACE THE EARLY PONY EXPRESS, TELEGRAPH AND RAILROAD ROUTES.

The greatest robbery of a Union Pacific train occurred at Big Springs the night of September 18, 1877. It was carried out by the Sam Bass gang. After capturing station agent John Barnhart and destroying the telegraph apparatus, the outlaws forced the express train to stop, stole $60,000 in gold coin, plus cash and jewelry from passengers, and then retreated under a lone tree to divide the loot. Bass and three others were tracked down; two were never caught.

DIXON COUNTY

COUNTY SEAT: PONCA • LICENSE PLATE PREFIX: 35 • POPULATION: 5,491
GOVERNED BY SEVEN COUNTY SUPERVISORS

Before 1850, Nebraska, particularly the area that would become Dixon County, was widely regarded as a "Great American Desert," characterized by its perceived lack of fertile soil, timber and potable water. It was also considered perilous because of local tribes' hostility toward each other.

However, the landscape began to change after Nebraska was designated a territory in 1854 and disputes with the Ponca Tribe were resolved. In 1858, legislator Downer T. Bramble spearheaded legislation to redraw Dakota County's boundaries to organize Dixon County and name it after Dixon's Bluff, which overlooks the Missouri River.

Ponca, established in 1856 and named in honor of the local indigenous peoples, won the county seat in 1858 after a contentious competition with North Bend and Concord. Despite ongoing challenges, by 1875 Ponca had become too dominant to be displaced by its rivals.

Today's Dixon County Courthouse is a blend of old and new. The original red brick structure dates to 1883-1884; the addition dates to 1940, built with assistance from the WPA.

The building is not handicap accessible and lacks sprinklers, leading to discussion about constructing a new facility. At the time of our visit, there was consideration of a bond issue, as well as the possibility of a private builder leasing a new structure back to the county.

Our tour began on the ground level, where the offices of elected officials and their vaults are furnished with period pieces and fixtures. The second-floor courtroom showcases a collection of photographs of county judges and the jury box features well-preserved 1940s oak swivel chairs. Adjacent to the courtroom, there's a law library and a jury room. On the third floor are the sheriff's office, dispatch center and jail facilities.

KICKSHAWS

Lewis and Clark camped near Dixon's Bluff during their westbound expedition in 1804.

Ponca State Park, situated on the banks of the Missouri River, was developed in 1934 by the Civilian Conservation Corps.

**DISPUTED SELECTION OF THE COUNTY SEAT UNTIL 1875
DELAYED CONSTRUCTION OF THE ORIGINAL COURTHOUSE TO 1883.**

DODGE COUNTY

COUNTY SEAT: FREMONT · LICENSE PLATE PREFIX: 5 · POPULATION: 37,187

GOVERNED BY SEVEN COUNTY SUPERVISORS

Dodge County is one of the eight original Nebraska counties, organized in 1855. It was named in honor of Augustus C. Dodge, a U.S. senator from Iowa. The county seat was named for John C. Fremont, a noted explorer who ran for president in 1856 when the town was platted.

Dodge County's expansive courthouse is the third to stand on the site, with both predecessors destroyed by fire.

The current four-story structure, designed by A.H. Dyer in the Neoclassical Revival style, features brick and Bedford stone and was completed in 1918 – a year after construction began. It has undergone several remodels and updates over the years and remains meticulously maintained.

The courthouse is connected to the Judicial Center via a skywalk, enhancing accessibility. Inside, the tile floors are striking, complemented by a grand staircase adorned with iron banisters and newel posts and marble wainscoting. County offices are spacious and functional; and the halls showcase local history through photos provided by the historical society, as well as loaned works.

Key areas include a board of supervisors meeting room designed for efficient business proceedings and citizen participation. The county courtroom is compact, while the Judicial Center houses several district courtrooms furnished in a modern style. Offices for CASA, Emergency Management and the Nebraska Mediation Center are also located in the courthouse.

Modern elevators enhance the aesthetic and functionality of the halls while the basement offers ample space for workshops, storage, utilities, and even houses a coal room (no longer in use).

KICKSHAWS

In 1872, Dodge County purchased 160 acres near Nickerson for a "poor farm" to provide relief for the needy. By 1888, the farm had grown to 245 acres. It was sold in 1955, after serving more than 400 residents.

WHEN BUILT, THE DODGE COUNTY COURTHOUSE PROVIDED JAILERS QUARTERS ON THE TOP FLOOR, WHICH CAN BE SEEN ON THE ORIGINAL BLUEPRINTS.

DOUGLAS COUNTY

COUNTY SEAT: OMAHA • LICENSE PLATE PREFIX: FORMERLY 1, NOW SIX-CHARACTER ALPHA-NUMERIC
POPULATION: 589,540 • GOVERNED BY SEVEN COUNTY COMMISSIONERS

The passage of the Kansas-Nebraska Act in 1854 granted territorial status to Kansas and Nebraska. The Nebraska Territorial Legislature subsequently established Omaha City and Douglas County the same year, naming the county in honor of Stephen A. Douglas, the Illinois senator who advocated for the bill. Within a year, Omaha was serving as the territorial capital.

The county's first courthouse, completed in 1858, was located at 15th and Douglas Streets. As Omaha grew and county business increased, a more substantial courthouse was erected at 17th and Farnam in 1885. This building was later demolished to make way for a grander structure designed by Omaha architect John Latenser and completed in 1912. His monumental design, in the French Renaissance Revival style, became Nebraska's largest courthouse.

While the exterior has largely retained its original design, the courthouse's interior has undergone significant updates and renovations. The most extensive project spanned 15 years and included restoration of the rotunda, skylight, stained-glass dome and eight-panel mural system on the fifth floor of the Hall of Justice.

The murals, created on canvas by William Rau and installed in 1912, illustrate the history and expansion of the United States and the Midwest. Over the years, the murals endured damage, neglect and numerous unsuccessful restoration attempts. By early 2009, their condition had become critical, prompting the Omaha Douglas Public Building Commission to spearhead a tedious restoration in collaboration with BVH Architecture and Evergreene Architectural Arts. The scaffolding came down in 2017 after two years of work on the murals.

The courthouse stands as one of Nebraska's premier examples of public art and was added to the National Register of Historic Places in 1979.

KICKSHAWS

Omaha and Douglas County have a cooperative city-county government model.

Douglas County employs approximately 2,500 people and operates a county health center and a county mental health center. It also has a freestanding Election Commission Office, one of four in the state.

COURTHOUSE LORE NOTES BUCKSHOT DAMAGE TO THE ROTUNDA'S MARBLE SURFACES, RESULTING FROM SHOTGUNS FIRED BY THE MOB DURING THE WILL BROWN LYNCHING.

In 1919, at the Douglas County Courthouse, a citizen mob lynched Will Brown, a Black man accused of assaulting a white woman. The same mob nearly succeeded in hanging Mayor Ed Smith and started fires causing more than $500,000 in damage to the courthouse. An historic marker on the courthouse lawn memorializes the event.

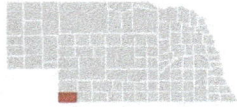

DUNDY COUNTY

COUNTY SEAT: BENKELMAN • LICENSE PLATE PREFIX: 76 • POPULATION: 1,561
GOVERNED BY THREE COUNTY COMMISSIONERS

Dundy County's boundaries were established in 1873, but it wasn't until nine years later, when settlers arrived with the railroad and the population grew to 200, that its governing body was formed.

The county is named after Elmer Dundy, the federal judge whose landmark 1879 decision in favor of Ponca Chief Standing Bear recognized Native Americans as "persons" under the law, marking a significant advancement in their legal rights.

Notable features include the tile floors, trimwork and classic iron stairs and newels. Offices and hallways showcase a blend of contemporary and vintage artwork, while the courtroom itself is simple yet functional.

During my visit, I coincidentally met County Clerk Miles Preston, who was adjusting to his new role and managing the aftermath of a sheriff's recall. At that time, he was the only male county clerk in Nebraska, a noteworthy detail given that county clerks were historically all men.

KICKSHAWS

Dundy County is situated in cattle and sheep country, where the predominant ground cover is buffalo grass.

Benkelman was originally named Collinsville until 1884.

MANY OF THE COURTHOUSE'S ORIGINAL FURNISHINGS AND FIXTURES REMAIN.

FILLMORE COUNTY

**COUNTY SEAT: GENEVA • LICENSE PLATE PREFIX: 34 • POPULATION: 5,548
GOVERNED BY SEVEN COUNTY SUPERVISORS**

Spring was budding when I returned to Geneva to explore the architecturally significant Fillmore County Courthouse.

Designed by George E. McDonald in the Richardsonian Romanesque style, the 1894 brick-and-stone building boasts tall arched windows and a striking 125-foot tower, modeled after the 1892 Gage County Courthouse in Beatrice. The tower's clocks, by W.P. McCall, were installed in 1909.

Fillmore County, established in 1856 and organized in 1871, was named for Millard Fillmore, the 13th president of the United States. As vice president, he assumed the presidency following the death of 12th U.S. President Zachary Taylor and completed Taylor's term.

The courthouse was listed on the National Register of Historic Places in the late 1970s. Its restoration by Berggren Architects, P.C., earned a prestigious 2002 Preservation Honors Award from the National Trust of Historic Places.

The restoration preserved the courthouse's distinctive interior tilework, oak woodwork, wallcoverings, wainscoting, decorative tin ceilings and a fireplace with glazed ceramic tiles and carved capitals and columns. Nineteenth-century gold-leaf office signage, photos of past county officials in the offices of the clerk and treasurer and handsomely presented artifacts, artwork, maps, flags and quilts all contribute to the museum-like atmosphere.

A grand wooden staircase ascends to the second floor, brightened by natural light streaming through a trio of tall windows. This floor houses the county and district court offices, driver's license exam area and library. The remodeled district courtroom features a domed ceiling and chandelier and walls lined with portraits of county and district court judges, including a notable 1953 photograph commemorating the first all-woman jury. The jury room is equipped with a buzzer system to notify the bailiff when a verdict is reached.

KICKSHAWS

Groups of cruising motorcyclists often stop in front of the courthouse to take pictures – a sight that makes courthouse personnel smile.

GENEVA WAS CHOSEN AS THE COUNTY SEAT FOR BEING THE GEOGRAPHICAL CENTER OF THE COUNTY.

Bootlegging proliferated in the county during Prohibition. This Thompson submachine gun was confiscated during a raid led by Sheriff Frank Steinacher, who served from 1930 to 1942. The courtroom was the site of several bootlegging-related trials.

FRANKLIN COUNTY

COUNTY SEAT: FRANKLIN • LICENSE PLATE PREFIX: 50 • POPULATION: 2,825
GOVERNED BY SEVEN COUNTY SUPERVISORS

Architect George A. Berlinghof designed the Franklin County Courthouse, completed in 1926, in the Classical Revival style. In all, Berlinghof has eight Nebraska courthouses to his credit.

The county was established in 1867, organized in 1871 and named after Benjamin Franklin, a founding father of the United States.

Initially, the county seat was Bloomington, which housed the United States Land Office until 1893. In 1920, voters moved the county seat to Franklin, a more populous town. During construction of the courthouse, the county board operated from a rented space.

Situated on a square block with minimalist landscaping, the three-story building maintains a straightforward, monument-like appearance. The interior retains much of its original furnishings and details, including plat tables, desks and chairs, etched-glass office doors, golden oak woodwork, brass light fixtures and terrazzo floors.

The first floor accommodates the sheriff's office, jail, driver's license exam room, Nebraska Extension and Veterans Services.

The second floor houses the offices of elected officials, tidy vaults and the county courtroom. The third floor contains a bright and spacious district courtroom with a vaulted ceiling, jury deliberation room and CASA office.

KICKSHAWS

Franklin County was one of the last to select its county seat. It went from Franklin to Bloomington and then back to Franklin in 1882 – 15 years after the county's establishment.

Before pioneers settled here, the area was a vast hunting ground for the Pawnee Tribe.

FRONTIER COUNTY

COUNTY SEAT: STOCKVILLE • LICENSE PLATE PREFIX: 60 • POPULATION: 2,585
GOVERNED BY THREE COUNTY COMMISSIONERS

Frontier County was established in 1872, at a time when it seemed to sit on the edge of civilization. The early settlers were primarily cattlemen, conducting business in a stock town that eventually became Stockville, the county seat.

The original courthouse was a wood-framed structure that was destroyed by fire in the early or mid-1890s (records differ on the year). It was replaced by the current two-story frame courthouse, flanked by two after-thought additions.

Stockville may have a population of just 15 residents today, but it serves as a vital center and social hub for various county services and those conducting other county business.

Walls and display cases on the first floor showcase paintings, prints, photos, commemorative flags, school trophies and a large plaque commemorating former county officials. Among them: Former Nebraska Gov. Frank Morrison, who began his law practice in Stockville and served as Frontier County attorney in 1934. On the second floor, a gallery is dedicated to the county's past superintendents of schools.

The county and district courts share a handsome courtroom furnished in rich golden oak. One of the most notable trials here was the so-called case of "The Hired Man" involving Eva Johnson and Harvey Durbin. In 1950, they were tried for the murder of Johnson's husband, Norval. The case involved an incident where gasoline was thrown on Norval Johnson as he went downstairs to check on a water heater. Both Eva Johnson and Durbin were found guilty. The bucket they allegedly used in the dousing remains in the courthouse, tagged as a trial exhibit.

KICKSHAWS

Stockville faced multiple county seat challenges from Curtis, beginning with the establishment of the railroad. County lore, according to The North Platte Telegraph, has a group of Curtis men riding horses south to Stockville, with the intention of looting records and bringing the county seat to Curtis by force, only to be met by armed Stockville men. County elections in 1920, 1930 and 1950 declared that Stockville remain the county seat.

FRONTIER COUNTY, AT 980 SQUARE MILES, IS MOSTLY GRASSLANDS AND "LIVESTOCK FRIENDLY."

This was the last courthouse in the nation to get indoor plumbing and a paved road leading to its doors. It also was one of the first counties in the state to be computerized, complete with property information on its website.

FURNAS COUNTY

COUNTY SEAT: BEAVER CITY • LICENSE PLATE PREFIX: 38 • POPULATION: 4,556
GOVERNED BY THREE COUNTY COMMISSIONERS

Furnas County was established in 1873 and named in honor of Robert W. Furnas, Nebraska's third governor, who played a key role in founding the Nebraska State Fair and Arbor Day.

In the early days of the county, a major dispute arose over the county seat, with Arapahoe and Beaver City competing for the title. The issue was ultimately resolved through a series of local votes and political negotiations.

In June 1867, Gen. George Armstrong Custer traveled through what is now Furnas County. He is perhaps best known for his role in the Battle of Little Bighorn in 1876, where he and his troops were defeated primarily by the Lakota Sioux, along with Cheyenne and Arapaho warriors.

The current courthouse, the second on the site, was designed by John Latenser of Omaha. Completed in 1949 and dedicated in 1951, it features buff-colored brick and stone in the Art Deco style.

The interior, characterized by wide halls, polished floors (some with geometric designs) and a mix of light and dark wood grains, was restored in 2016.

The first floor houses the offices of the county court, magistrate, county attorney and sheriff, and the jail.

The second floor accommodates various county services, including Nebraska Emergency Management, planning and zoning, driver's license examining and Nebraska Extension.

The third floor features the office of the clerk of district court and a spacious, modern district courtroom. Notable elements include a wood accent behind the bench and green-and-black checkerboard floor tile in the gallery.

KICKSHAWS

In Nebraska, 88 of 93 counties have election commissioners, a role typically held by one of the elected officers, usually the county clerk. Five of the state's larger counties – Douglas, Lancaster, Sarpy, Hall and Buffalo – have a dedicated election commissioner separate from other county offices.

GAGE COUNTY

COUNTY SEAT: BEATRICE • LICENSE PLATE PREFIX: 3 • POPULATION: 21,634
GOVERNED BY SEVEN COUNTY SUPERVISORS

Building Supervisor Dave Jones provided a wealth of historical information as he guided us through Beatrice's Richardsonian Romanesque courthouse designed by Louis Gunn and Frederick Curtiss of Kansas City, Missouri.

The Grand Lodge of Masons of Nebraska laid the cornerstone in 1890; two years later, the limestone landmark was ready for occupancy. Established in 1855, the county was named for Rev. William D. Gage, the first Methodist pastor in Nebraska and chaplain of the first territorial legislature. The Homestead Act of 1862 attracted scores of settlers to the area for free land.

A fire in 1960 caused significant damage to the courthouse, leading to extensive restoration and renovation. During the renovation, a coffered ceiling in the county courtroom was discovered, hidden behind ceiling tiles for decades. The building's most recent update was in 2008.

Much of the original grandeur is preserved, starting with the black-and-white checkerboard floor tile in the main hallway. The district courtroom is particularly impressive with its soaring, dark oak coffered ceiling, dramatic floor-to-ceiling arched windows, engraved cornices and decorative wood behind the bench. The furniture, locally crafted by Ratigan-Schottler, is equally commanding.

The commissioner's meeting room has numerous paintings and murals by Dee Johnson supported by the Gage County Historical Society and Museum and the Beatrice Public Library. During a subsequent visit, this room was a prep area for materials for voting precincts in Gage County.

Each December, the courthouse is outlined in holiday lights, a tradition that attracts visitors from miles around.

KICKSHAWS

The Gage County Courthouse is mentioned in Laura Ingalls Wilder's "On the Way Home," a chronicle of her family's journey from South Dakota to Missouri. Her diary mentions passing through Beatrice on August 5, 1894.

Without the persuasive efforts of F.W. Carstens, the fire-damaged courthouse might have been lost to demolition. It also helped that prisoners at the time knew how to hang dry wall.

THE TOWER STILL FEATURES ITS ORIGINAL BELL AND A CLOCK SOURCED FROM THE POST OFFICE.

GARDEN COUNTY

COUNTY SEAT: OSHKOSH • **LICENSE PLATE PREFIX: 77** • **POPULATION: 1,794**
GOVERNED BY THREE COUNTY COMMISSIONERS

A year of touring Nebraska's courthouses concluded in Oshkosh on December 7, 2023.

Many of today's counties were carved out of larger counties. Such was the case with Garden County, which separated from northern Deuel County following an election in November 1909. It's name comes from early settlers who believed the county would become "the Garden Spot of the West."

Oshkosh's two-story courthouse, built in 1921 in the Classical Revival style, was listed on the National Register of Historic Places in 1990. A significant update included the addition of a west wing to provide elevator access.

On the main level, you'll find the offices of elected officials, many featuring original oak counters and vaults. The county commissioners' boardroom, along with offices for Nebraska Extension and probation services, are also located on this floor.

The second floor houses the offices of the county and district courts and the county attorney. The courtrooms are bright and welcoming, featuring warm wood grain on the judge's bench and bar and period theater chairs with under-seat hat racks in the gallery.

The lower level is dedicated to the sheriff's office and jail, allowing for efficient management of prisoners until their court appearance.

KICKSHAWS

The courthouse square was a pivotal factor in the selection of the county seat, as towns developed around it. Wealthy citizens donated land, railroads contributed to the establishment of the square, land companies reserved and often donated the space to the county, and early bond issues were sold to fund its creation.

THE COURTROOM FEATURES ANTIQUE
SWIVEL CHAIRS IN THE JURY BOX.

GARFIELD COUNTY

COUNTY SEAT: BURWELL • LICENSE PLATE PREFIX: 83 • POPULATION: 1,763
GOVERNED BY THREE COUNTY COMMISSIONERS

Garfield County, established in 1884, originally had its county seat in Willow Springs. The seat was moved to Burwell when the railroad arrived.

The county is named after James A. Garfield, the 20th president of the United States, who served from 1881 until his assassination in September of the same year.

The courthouse, the third on the site, was constructed in 1962 by the Grand Island firm of Thomas, Benjamin & Clayton.

Inside, you'll find the usual county offices along hallways with random avocado-and-redwood slate tile flooring and reddish-brown brick walls accented with eye-catching turquoise tile. Among the historical photos, maps and quilts, a tourism slogan brings a smile: "Nebraska, The Good Life."

Watching over the double doors to the courtroom is a large tile mosaic of Lady Justice. The courtroom, designed in a midcentury modern style, is complemented by comfortable jury seating and beautiful walnut wood paneling extending behind the bench.

The one-level building is clean and well-maintained. Notably, it does not include a jail facility; instead, the county contracts with Valley County for jail services.

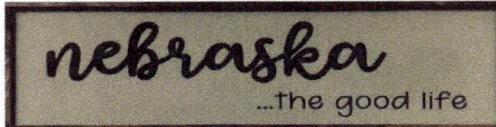

KICKSHAWS

Sioux and Pawnee tribal conflicts occurred in the area in 1874 and 1876.

THE NORTH LOUP AND CALAMUS RIVERS COME TOGETHER IN GARFIELD COUNTY.

GOSPER COUNTY

COUNTY SEAT: ELWOOD • LICENSE PLATE PREFIX: 73 • POPULATION: 1,847
GOVERNED BY THREE COUNTY COMMISSIONERS

Gosper County was established in 1873 and named after John J. Gosper, Nebraska's third secretary of state.

The current courthouse, completed in 1939, is Elwood's fourth. Designed by McClure and Wallace of Kearney, nearly half of the construction costs were covered by the WPA.

The courthouse replaced a frame structure that burned in 1895, resulting in the loss of some records. Gosper's "Boot County" nickname arose because of Muddy Township's odd extension into Frontier County, for reasons that remain unclear.

The courthouse's public areas have glazed brick walls and glass block accents. Original door hardware and light fixtures are preserved and a chair lift ensures accessibility. The walls display maps, prints, a cast brass plate noting the courthouse's WPA origins and a sign bearing "In God We Trust."

The first floor features office space for elected officials, each with their own vaults. Among the historic artifacts is an early 20th-century ballot box, on display in the clerk's office. In a modern sign of the times, the DMV was "closed due to staffing shortages."

The second floor houses the county courtroom, the district courtroom, the transit office and the sheriff's office. Jail services are contracted with Dawson County. The basement, used for storage, is accessed by a circular stair.

KICKSHAWS

Johnson Lake State Recreation Area six miles north of Elwood is a popular destination for camping, fishing and water sports.

Elwood became the fourth county seat location, a result of the railroad's routing.

THE COUNTY COURTROOM IS UNUSED BECAUSE GOSPER AND DAWSON COUNTIES SHARE A JUDGE.

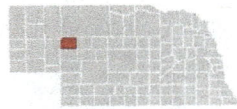

GRANT COUNTY

COUNTY SEAT: HYANNIS • LICENSE PLATE PREFIX: 92 • POPULATION: 565
GOVERNED BY THREE COUNTY BOARD MEMBERS

You know you're in a "Livestock Friendly County" when you arrive in Hyannis, deep in the Sand Hills. The slogan "God's Cow Country" is proudly displayed throughout town, including the exterior of the Grant County Courthouse.

In a county established in 1887 and named after 18th U.S. President Ulysses S. Grant, the campaign highlights the importance of cattle ranching to the local economy.

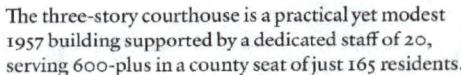

The three-story courthouse is a practical yet modest 1957 building supported by a dedicated staff of 20, serving 600-plus in a county seat of just 165 residents.

The building is fully accessible and built to last with marble floors, stairs and trim. The lower level houses the local library, while the main floor accommodates county officials, document vaults and the sheriff's office.

The second floor includes a modest district courtroom with midcentury paneling and furnishings, plus the Grant County Museum, open by appointment.

The main floor displays a collection of art, historical documents and artifacts – many of which are on loan from the Metcalf family, early settlers of the area.

KICKSHAWS

Grant County, which is situated in the Mountain Time Zone, is the ninth least-populous county in the United States.

In 1954, the Nebraska Sand Hills became a designated National Natural Landmark for its distinctive rolling sand dunes, rich grasslands and diverse ecosystems.

The Whitman murder trial is a notable event in the county's history. The trial centered on the murder of William Whitman, a local rancher, in the early 1900s. The main suspect in the case was Jesse T. Williams, a local resident. The guilty verdict was significant for its impact on local law and order and the community's sense of justice.

Nebraska has 35 counties officially designated as Livestock Friendly Counties by the Nebraska Department of Agriculture.

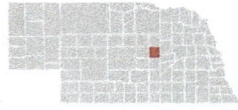

GREELEY COUNTY

COUNTY SEAT: GREELEY • LICENSE PLATE PREFIX: 62 • POPULATION: 2,219
GOVERNED BY THREE COUNTY COMMISSIONERS

Greeley County was named in honor of Horace Greeley, founder and editor of The New York Tribune. He popularized the phrase, "Go west, young man, go west."

The current county seat, in the geographical center of the county, wasn't established until 1890.

When the county was organized in 1872, the initial county seat was Lamartine. In 1874, residents of Scotia held another election and won the designation. Eventually, Greeley was chosen due to its central location and advantageous railroad connections.

The Greeley County Courthouse, designed in the Classical Revival style by architect George Berlinghof of Berlinghof & Davis in Lincoln, stands four stories tall. Construction began in 1913 with the laying of the cornerstone; the building was completed in 1914. This courthouse replaced a smaller brick structure, which had become inadequate and was condemned in 1910.

The courthouse is a less elaborate version of the Howard County Courthouse built in 1912-15. The bond issue passed by just one vote. Berlinghof's design, noted for its modernity and simplicity, remains largely unaltered. Original features include terrazzo flooring in the halls and marble counters in offices. A striking aspect is the use of white marble for wainscoting, stairs and elegantly curved banisters.

The second-story district courtroom retains its original high ceiling, broad plaster beams and pairs of unadorned pilasters between long narrow windows. The room features white marble mopboards and simple wood furnishings from Wollaeger Manufacturing, as noted in the courthouse's entry on the National Register of Historic Places. On the third floor, the old jail and two sequestered jury rooms – one for men and one for women – serve as reminders of the past.

KICKSHAWS

In 1885, Greeley was set to be called "Spading," but the name was rejected by the postal service because of its similarity to "Spalding," another town in the county.

In the 1920s, Greeley boasted its largest-ever population, at more than 900 residents (400 today). Many of its early settlers hailed from Ireland.

LOCAL LORE INCLUDES TALES OF A GHOST HAUNTING THE COURTHOUSE, SAID TO BE THE SPIRIT OF SOMEONE WHO DIED IN THE JAIL.

HALL COUNTY

COUNTY SEAT: GRAND ISLAND • LICENSE PLATE PREFIX: 8 • POPULATION: 62,197
GOVERNED BY SEVEN COUNTY COMMISSIONERS

Hall County, established in 1858 and named after Augustus Hall of Bellevue, chief justice of the Nebraska Territory (1858-1861), continues to use its original courthouse. Completed in 1904, it was designed by Omaha architect Thomas R. Kimball in the Beaux-Arts style.

The building, distinguished by its striking red brick with limestone accents, is fully accessible amid iron-and-wood staircases with decorative newels. The ground floor boasts an impressive marble inlay with a geometric design. The centerpiece of the courthouse is an open rotunda, crowned by a stained-glass skylight that floods the space with natural light.

The courtrooms are bright, spacious and well-appointed, having been periodically updated to meet modern needs. They encircle the rotunda and open onto decorative walkways with marble drinking fountains and intricate wall and ceiling details.

One block east of the courthouse is the Hall County Administration Building, which was erected in 1980. It houses the offices of elected officials and the county's document vaults.

Significant changes, however, are on the horizon. In April 2024, the county commissioners voted to move forward on a multimillion-dollar revamp to preserve the original courthouse while updating the justice space and expanding the number of courtrooms to meet growing demand. The architect's proposal includes a skywalk connecting the old and new structures, with construction expected to be completed by summer 2027.

KICKSHAWS

Seventy-one of Nebraska's 93 counties use the county commissioner method of local governance. Commissioners are elected by their respective districts.

The county has a freestanding election commission.

Hall County is home to the Stuhr Museum of the Prairie Pioneer. Located in Grand Island, the museum highlights the westward migration.

GRAND ISLAND IS KNOWN FOR ITS LOCATION ALONG INTERSTATE 80, THE PLATTE RIVER AND THE CENTRAL FLYWAY FOR CRANES MIGRATING THROUGH NEBRASKA.

HAMILTON COUNTY

COUNTY SEAT: AURORA • LICENSE PLATE PREFIX: 28 • POPULATION: 9,537
GOVERNED BY FIVE COUNTY COMMISSIONERS

Administrative Manager Scott Stuhr escorted me through the corridors of Aurora's picturesque Hamilton County Courthouse. Dating to 1895, the cherished landmark is a striking example of Richardsonian Romanesque architecture, characterized by its central tower and robust red brick and sandstone facade. Often described as County Capitol style, the well-maintained building has undergone several renovations, yet it maintains its historic integrity.

Designed by William Gray of Lincoln, this courthouse is the third for Hamilton County. Organized in 1870 and named after Alexander Hamilton, the first secretary of the U.S. treasury, the county originally had its county seat in Orville City. The move to Aurora in 1877 was fiercely contested, but after five ballots, Aurora emerged victorious.

Accessible and elegantly appointed, the courthouse features wide hallways with beautiful decorative tile flooring, unique white oak wainscoting, trim, stairways and intricately carved newel posts. Notably, it includes a Veterans Memorial Tower.

Walls are adorned with maps, photos, displays and a centennial quilt commemorating the courthouse. The period woodwork, doors, hardware, furnishings and marble water fountain from the 1890s contribute to the building's historical authenticity. The second-floor landing is particularly notable for its cathedral windows.

The lower level houses Nebraska Extension, the DMV and Veterans Services. The main floor accommodates the offices of elected officials, probation officers and the county surveyor. The top floor includes courtrooms, a jury room with tall windows and a well-maintained vault. The district courtroom is spacious, featuring a handsome white oak-paneled judge's bench, an ornate curved bar and original wooden jury chairs complete with hat racks.

KICKSHAWS

The top level of the central tower features strobe lights illuminated at night in memory of Dr. Harold Edgerton, an Aurora native who did pioneering work in high-speed photography and strobe lighting.

Originally, there was a caretaker's residence on the lower level.

THE COURTHOUSE IS VISIBLE FROM VARIOUS VANTAGE POINTS IN TOWN AS WELL AS FROM SEVERAL MILES OUT IN THE SURROUNDING COUNTRYSIDE.

HARLAN COUNTY

COUNTY SEAT: ALMA • LICENSE PLATE PREFIX: 51 • POPULATION: 3,045
GOVERNED BY SEVEN COUNTY SUPERVISORS

The person who likely knows the most about the Harlan County Courthouse – the maintenance man – took me on an informative tour.

Built between 1964 and 1966, this single-story midcentury modern building was designed by Thomas Benjamin Clayton Architects of Grand Island. It is the second courthouse on this site.

The first point of interest on our walkabout was a 12-foot-by-18-foot inlaid tile depiction of the Harlan County Reservoir on the floor just outside the district courtroom. The reservoir is a vital resource for water management, recreation and economic support in the area.

Harlan County, formed in 1871 from Lincoln County, may have been named after James Harlan, the U.S. secretary of the interior in the mid-1880s, or a revenue collector named Harlan who lived near the Republican River. Local historians just aren't sure!

Following several elections and a district judge's ruling, Alma became the county seat, with records eventually moved from the original seat, Melrose.

The courthouse is spacious and functional, accommodating all elected officials, their document storage vaults and a large assembly room for community meetings. It also includes the DMV, courtroom, judges' offices, law library and a jury room. Offices for the road and weed departments and the county surveyor are on the lower level.

The courtroom offers open, well-appointed spaces with warm wood paneling and furnishings consistent with its midcentury construction. A small bronze sculpture of Lady Justice crowns a bookcase behind the judge's bench.

KICKSHAWS

An early judge left pithy judicial statements in Latin on the wall of his office, which have been preserved.

The area was settled by German immigrants.

Twenty-two of Nebraska counties govern through a township board of supervisors structure.

THE REPUBLICAN RIVER FLOWS THROUGH PART OF HARLAN COUNTY.

HAYES COUNTY

COUNTY SEAT: HAYES CENTER • LICENSE PLATE PREFIX: 79 • POPULATION: 846
GOVERNED BY THREE COUNTY COMMISSIONERS

For centuries, vast herds of buffalo roamed Hayes County, hunted by American Indian tribes. In the 1800s, Buffalo Bill Cody and other hunters provided buffalo meat to workers constructing the Union Pacific Railroad. In 1872, Nebraska hosted Russian Grand Duke Alexis for a grand hunt with Chief Spotted Tail and the Brulé Lakota Sioux. A red marble marker inside the courthouse in Hayes Center commemorates the hunt.

Originally part of Shorter County, which covered much of southwestern Nebraska, the area was first known as Lincoln County before Hayes County was created in 1877 and organized in 1884.

Named in honor of 19th U.S. President Rutherford B. Hayes, the county saw the Texas Cattle Trail pass through its western region in the 1880s, enroute to the Ogallala railhead for delivery to major markets. The cattle were purchased to feed the Sioux per a treaty with the federal government, as the buffalo were all but extinguished.

These and other historic touchstones may be found by browsing the Hayes County Historical Society Museum, located on the lower level of the two-story courthouse.

The main floor houses the county's elected officials, with additional duties assigned to the clerk and treasurer. It also includes vaults, meeting rooms and corridors lined with paintings of the American West and old-time prints, maps, photos, calendars and signs.

The second floor features a modern courtroom, finished in blonde woodwork, along with a jury room and offices for court personnel.

KICKSHAWS

Hayes Center was once known as the "Windmill City," because each home had its own windmill-fed water supply, and a public windmill with a tank was situated in the middle of Main Street.

The town's biggest events are the Hayes County Fair and a community Fourth of July celebration.

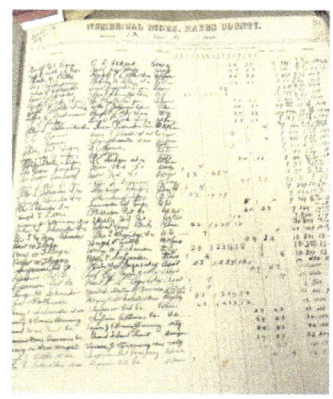  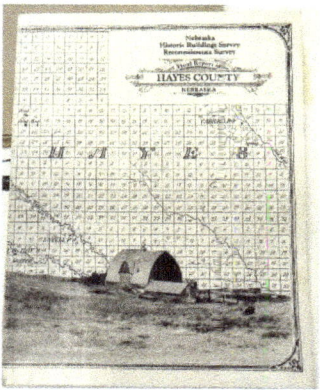

IT'S SAID THAT HAYES COUNTY IS THE MIDDLE OF NOWHERE, BUT THE CENTER OF EVERYWHERE.

HITCHCOCK COUNTY

COUNTY SEAT: TRENTON • LICENSE PLATE PREFIX: 67 • POPULATION: 2,552
GOVERNED BY THREE COUNTY COMMISSIONERS

The Hitchcock County Courthouse in Trenton, built in 1969 with funds from inheritance taxes, stands on the same ground as its predecessor, which explains the expansive front lawn.

The county, encompassing the Republican and Frenchman River valleys, was organized by the Nebraska Legislature in 1873. It is named after Phineas Warren Hitchcock, a lawyer, surveyor-general and U.S. senator from Nebraska.

Before Trenton was established, two post offices – Trail and Trail City – were set up along the Great Western Cattle Trail. Trenton obtained its post office in 1884.

Trenton wasn't the original county seat. Culbertson had the distinction for 20 years, from 1886 to 1893, during the era of huge Texas cattle drives through southwest Nebraska. In 1893, the county seat was moved to Trenton, near the center of the county.

The layout of Trenton's single-story courthouse is open and functional, featuring offices in vaults. The district courtroom is decorated with maps, flags, veterans memorial plaques, prints and etchings. A painting in the main hallway reflecting Native American heritage adds a touch of local pride.

KICKSHAWS

Driving west, Hitchcock County is the last Nebraska county in the Central Time Zone.

In August 1873, the Battle of Massacre Canyon occurred just 3 miles east of Trenton. A Pawnee hunting party of about 700 was caught in a devasting surprise attack by a Sioux war party. The conflict continued until a cavalry unit arrived.

HOLT COUNTY

COUNTY SEAT: O'NEILL • LICENSE PLATE PREFIX: 36 • POPULATION: 10,093
GOVERNED BY SEVEN COUNTY SUPERVISORS

In October 2023, I visited O'Neill, the Irish Capital of Nebraska, to explore the Holt County Courthouse.

Organized in 1876, the county is named after Joseph Holt of Kentucky, a prominent figure who served as postmaster general, secretary of war and judge advocate general of the Army.

O'Neill was chosen as the county seat in 1879 after a special election and faced several challenges but held its position. The town was founded in 1874 by Gen. John O'Neill, an Irish immigrant and American Civil War veteran.

The courthouse, constructed with Federal Emergency Administration of Public Works funds in 1936, received a significant addition and remodeling in 2005.

The first level contains offices for elected officials and their vaults. The floor features inlaid geometric designs, and the walls are decorated with maps, flags, throws, posters, prints and photos.

The second level includes the district courtroom, its associated offices, an extensive law library and a jury room. The district courtroom retains its original woodwork, stained gray, giving it a distinctive appearance. Notably, this floor also has a Problem Solving Court. A mounted longhorn steer head on the second floor reflects the region's heritage as a Livestock Friendly County. The third floor houses the sheriff's office and the county jail.

The basement is home to the county court, county judge and public defender's offices. The courtroom is modern and well-appointed. The courthouse's attractive features include distinctive stairs with unique newel post landings and glazed gray brick windowsills. It's a well-maintained facility with a blend of historical charm and modern functionality.

KICKSHAWS

A county treasurer in the late 1800s embezzled taxpayer dollars and did time at the state penitentiary. A governor commuted his sentence after five years. On a New Year's Eve buggy ride with his family, the former treasurer was grabbed by vigilantes. His body was found under the ice of the Niobrara River.

THE COUNTY, WHICH IS 67 PERCENT GRASSLAND,
RANKS NO. 2 IN THE U.S. FOR BEEF COWS, PER THE DROVERS REPORT.

HOOKER COUNTY

COUNTY SEAT: MULLEN • LICENSE PLATE PREFIX: 93 • POPULATION: 679
GOVERNED BY THREE COUNTY COMMISSIONERS

Hooker County, organized in 1889, was named after Civil War Gen. Joseph Hooker. Its current courthouse has remained largely unchanged since its construction in 1912.

The county clerk, who also serves as the election commissioner and clerk of the district court, introduced me to the building and even to a retired clerk who stopped by to say hello.

The red brick structure houses all the usual county offices. The district courtroom features original furniture, woodwork, doors and light fixtures. The basement, which once contained 19th-century steel jail cells, now serves as storage.

A highlight of the day was talking with a fixture in county government, centenarian Frank E. Harding, a lifelong resident of Mullen who had served as a county commissioner for more than 30 years and had remained active in history and Government Day presentations to high school students. Mr. Harding died at age 102 on March 26, 2024, a few months after our conversation.

KICKSHAWS

Hooker County is one of Nebraska's most productive cattle-raising regions.

Motorists frequently stop to have their photos taken in front of the Hooker County sign on Nebraska Highway 2.

The Mullen County courtroom was the setting for a notorious murder and fraudulent land claims case. The newly created FBI, under President Theodore Roosevelt, was involved, marking it as one of the agency's earliest cases.

MULLEN IS THE ONLY TOWN IN HOOKER COUNTY.

HOWARD COUNTY

COUNTY SEAT: ST. PAUL • LICENSE PLATE PREFIX: 49 • POPULATION: 6,527
GOVERNED BY THREE COUNTY COMMISSIONERS

Howard County was established in 1871 and named after Civil War Gen. Oliver Otis Howard. The courthouse was constructed of limestone and brick from 1912 to 1915. It stands out for its monumental proportions and grand architectural design.

The project, which went over budget, was designed by Lincoln architect George Berlinghof, known for his Classical Revival style. Berlinghof later applied this same style to smaller courthouses in Greeley and Franklin.

Of special note is a women's restroom, intended as a "nice resting place for those who will come to the county seat from a distance," according to a 1915 newspaper article.

The first floor also originally featured an assembly room dedicated to the Grand Army of the Republic, a fraternal organization for Union veterans of the Civil War. This historical connection is commemorated with the statue of a Union Army veteran on the south lawn.

The interior boasts a range of well-preserved architectural details, including marble stairs and balusters, coffered ceilings, ornamental plasterwork, terrazzo floors and single-pane transoms with painted office designations.

The second floor houses vaults and offices for elected county officials and magistrates for district and county court. The hallways are furnished with period benches and chairs and feature displays of historical artifacts, including a General Land Office survey map.

The top floor has offices for the sheriff and district judge, and the spacious courtroom, notable for its ornate cornice, fanciful lion heads, classical motifs and ceiling fixtures adorned with gold-accented medallions.

KICKSHAWS

Immigrant groups from Denmark, Bohemia, Germany and Poland were among the early settlers.

St. Paul narrowly staved off Dannebrog's attempt to be the county seat.

Worth visiting: The Howard County Historical Village, one block east of the courthouse.

HOWARD COUNTY'S TREASURED LANDMARK JOINED THE NATIONAL REGISTER OF HISTORIC PLACES IN 1990.

HOWARD COUNTY IS PART OF THE GRAND ISLAND METROPOLITAN STATISTICAL AREA.

JEFFERSON COUNTY

COUNTY SEAT: FAIRBURY • **LICENSE PLATE PREFIX: 33** • **POPULATION: 7,054**
GOVERNED BY THREE COUNTY COMMISSIONERS

Jefferson County was carved out of Jones County in 1871 and named in honor of third U.S. President Thomas Jefferson.

The courthouse was designed by J.G. Holland of Topeka, Kansas, and completed in 1892 as a striking example of Richardsonian Romanesque architecture, marked by a square domed tower with a four-faced clock and statues depicting Justice, Law and Freedom. The stone used in the construction was sourced locally and cut by hand by English stonecutters living in Fairbury.

The courthouse has undergone several remodels, most recently in 2016. The ground floor boasts well-maintained gray-and-white marble floors and handsome transom-style office doors.

The first floor hosts the offices of elected officials, their vaults and a DMV area. This floor features original wood floors, radiators and service counters, plus preserved fireplaces with decorative tilework. The woodwork and doors remain original, and the wooden stairs are notable for their intricate rails and newel posts. Hallways are decorated with military tributes and artifacts, including a Gatling gun. Some century-old chairs are still in use.

The second floor houses the district court, county court and probation offices. The district courtroom stands out for its ornate wrought-iron gallery seats, though the jury box has been updated.

KICKSHAWS

The Rock Island Railroad Depot, a notable example of early 20th-century architecture, offers a glimpse into Fairbury's rich history and the vital role that railroads played in its development.

Rock Creek, a significant Pony Express and Oregon-California Trail station in Nebraska, is located east of Fairbury. In July 1861, it was the site of an incident in which Wild Bill Hickok shot and killed station attendant David McCames during a dispute.

THE TOWER CLOCK, AFFECTIONATELY CALLED "LITTLE BEN," WAS INSTALLED IN 1910 AND TOLLS ON THE HOUR.

JOHNSON COUNTY

COUNTY SEAT: TECUMSEH • LICENSE PLATE PREFIX: 57 • POPULATION: 5,198

GOVERNED BY THREE COUNTY COMMISSIONERS

The names of Johnson County and its county seat are closely intertwined. The county seat is named after the Shawnee Chief Tecumseh, who was killed by Richard Mentor Johnson in a hand-to-hand struggle during the War of 1812. Johnson, an Army officer, was the ninth vice president of the United States under Martin Van Buren.

William Gray was the architect of the courthouse, which was built in the Romanesque Revival style in 1889. It is the county's third courthouse to occupy the square since the county was organized in 1857.

Renovations between 2000 and 2002 seamlessly blended old and new, preserving the landmark's 19th-century tin ceilings, arched alcoves, vaults and transom doors with ornamental mouldings.

Twenty years later, the courthouse is undergoing another major update to reconfigure existing spaces, improve accessibility and enhance efficiency for those who use the building daily. The largest phase of the project, completed in 2024, repurposed the former clerk of court's office into two courtrooms, including a large magistrate courtroom. Other additions included judge and court reporter offices and a multipurpose space for jury deliberations.

During my visit, the lower levels housed elected officials and their vaults, while the upper level contained the district courtroom, court offices, law library and jury room. The courtroom was well-lit and crisply updated along with the rest of the building with white-painted woodwork.

Gray, the architect, also designed the courthouses in Cass, Hamilton, York and Butler counties and submitted plans for the Lancaster County Courthouse. His other claim to fame? He invented the pressure cooker.

KICKSHAWS

The Johnson County Historical Society makes its home in a former church built in 1889.

On the Fourth of July, hundreds of American flags adorn the courthouse square.

A good friend of the author was married here.

THE BROWNVILLE-FORT KEARNY TRAIL RAN THROUGH THE COUNTY.

KEARNEY COUNTY

COUNTY SEAT: MINDEN • LICENSE PLATE PREFIX: 52 • POPULATION: 6,770
GOVERNED BY SEVEN COUNTY COMMISSIONERS

Established in 1860 and finalized in its current form in 1873, the Kearney County Courthouse was named after Fort Kearny and Maj. Gen. Stephen Watts Kearny, an important military leader in the expansion of the American West.

The cornerstone for the courthouse was laid by the Masonic Grand Lodge in 1906, and the building was completed in 1907. Designed by George Berlinghof in the Classical Revival style, it resembles his Seward County Courthouse, which was dedicated just two years earlier. Minden's courthouse features a steel-framed central bell tower, marking a departure from the wooden towers of the late 1800s.

Despite some remodeling, including the addition of an elevator, the courthouse retains its historic integrity.

Black-and-white checkerboard marble flooring that extends throughout the building, complemented by the main staircase with its black iron rails and newel posts. Additionally, much of the oak furniture remains original, crafted by John Fastje of Denison, Iowa.

The first floor offices include Nebraska Extension, the county attorney, child support services and emergency management. The walls are adorned with prints, maps, signs and a display of two Civil War Gatling guns. The second floor of the courthouse contains the offices of the elected officials and their vaults, with circular metal stairs providing typical access to additional storage.

On the third floor is the county court, district court, district judge's office, law library and jury room. The courtroom details include a decorative tin ceiling, brass globe chandelier and a Scales of Justice relief carving on the face of the judge's bench. The sheriff's department and four other county offices are housed in a nearby building.

KICKSHAWS

U.S. Sen. Carl T. Curtis was born in Kearney County. His tenure, from 1954 to 1979, made him one of the longest-serving senators in the state's history. He died August 28, 2000, at 94.

Prior to 1878, Kearney City was the county seat.

The county has a ghost town – Dobytown. It experienced a decline as transportation and economic conditions changed, leading to abandonment.

THE COURTHOUSE IS ESPECIALLY WORTH A VISIT WHEN "THE CHRISTMAS CITY" LIGHTS UP WITH THOUSANDS OF HOLIDAY LIGHTS. IT WAS A PIONEER IN THIS TRADITION, LEADING THE COMMUNITY IN INSTALLING HOLIDAY DECORATIONS AS EARLY AS 1915.

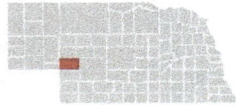

KEITH COUNTY

COUNTY SEAT: OGALLALA • LICENSE PLATE PREFIX: 68 • POPULATION: 8,113
GOVERNED BY FIVE COUNTY COMMISSIONERS

Keith County, established in 1873, had no permanent settlement until the railroad arrived in 1867. The county is named after early rancher Morrell C. Keith, whose grandson Keith Neville was elected governor of Nebraska in 1917. The county seat was named for Crazy Horse, the Oglala Lakota war leader who led the first charge on Custer during the Battle of the Little Bighorn.

Despite the county's rich historical background, the courthouse itself is a product of the mid-20th century. Designed by the architectural firm Hinde & Laurinat, the 1962 building features a clean, modern aesthetic with blonde woodwork and furniture.

The facility is well-suited to its functions, and through an interlocal agreement, Keith County also provides court and jail services for nearby Arthur County.

The upper floor of the courthouse houses the district courtroom, featuring a quote above the entry that reads, "Laws are the very bulwarks of Liberty, they define every man's rights and defend the individual liberties of all men." This courtroom, along with the offices of elected officials and their vaults, forms the core of the courthouse's operations.

The basement accommodates several essential services, including the clerk of the district court, county surveyor, assessor, human resources and planning and zoning. The sheriff's office and jail have a separate entrance.

Noteworthy details include an antique Seth Thomas clock, art made from old license plates and a collection of official seals.

KICKSHAWS

Home of Lake McConaughy, Nebraska's largest body of water covering 30,000 surface acres.

The Union Pacific Railroad traversed the county in 1868.

BOTH THE OREGON AND MORMON TRAILS CROSSED THROUGH KEITH COUNTY.

KEYA PAHA COUNTY

COUNTY SEAT: SPRINGVIEW • LICENSE PLATE PREFIX: 82 • POPULATION: 805
GOVERNED BY THREE COUNTY COMMISSIONERS

Keya Paha, pronounced "kip-a-haw," is derived from the Dakota language, meaning "Turtle Hill," a name inspired by the small, rounded hills in the area. Organized in 1885, it was initially part of Dakota Territory before being transferred to Nebraska in 1882.

Constructed in 1914, the two-story courthouse lacks accessibility features. County officials have adapted by designating the main floor for offices, vaults and meeting space. The hallway showcases a large painting of early Springview by a local artist and a bronze plaque recognizing donors to the Keya Paha County Foundation.

The district courtroom on the second floor is modest, featuring a raised judge's bench and accent paneling. The courthouse floor is finished with small ivory hexagon tiles bordered by a geometric corn mosaic pattern in gray, tan and green square tiles.

The basement houses the weed superintendent's office and storage. Its garden-level windows are of glass block, blending functionality with design.

KICKSHAWS

In its early years, Springview earned the nickname "Mob County" as vigilantes pursued notorious outlaws like Doc Middleton and Kid Wade, who robbed the Burton bank, stole horses and hid in the canyons along the Niobrara River.

Keya Paha County is the most Republican-voting county in Nebraska, with Woodrow Wilson being the last Democratic presidential candidate to win there in 1916.

THE COUNTY IS HOME TO THE NIOBRARA NATIONAL SCENIC RIVER, A DESIGNATED NATIONAL PROTECTED AREA.

KIMBALL COUNTY

COUNTY SEAT: KIMBALL • LICENSE PLATE PREFIX: 71 • POPULATION: 3,289
GOVERNED BY THREE COUNTY COMMISSIONERS

Kimball County, established in 1888 from Cheyenne County, is named after Thomas Lord Kimball, vice president and general manager of Union Pacific Railroad and father of Nebraska architect Thomas R. Kimball.

Situated at Nebraska's western edge, the county borders Wyoming to the west and Colorado to the south. The area is predominantly agricultural with tillable soil, contrasting with the Sand Hills to the east.

The courthouse, designed by E.L. Goldsmith and completed in 1928, is built in the Classical Revival style. Its exterior is clad in Carthage stone, while the interior features Ozark gray marble complemented by walnut and oak woodwork. Notably, some of the marble flooring contains fossils.

On the first floor, you'll find the commissioners' room, the treasurer's office (with an impressive collection of old license plates), the DMV, Veterans Services and an assembly room. The second floor houses the county clerk's office with a large vault and circular metal stairs leading to additional storage, as well as the county judge's and assessor's offices. The hallways are lined with displays, antique benches, paintings, veterans memorials and maps.

The third floor is dedicated to the sheriff's office and the district courtroom, which includes the clerk of the district court's office, a large vault and a jury room. The law library boasts numerous volumes, with some lining the rear of the courtroom. The courtroom and jury box are spacious, illuminated by original light fixtures from the 1920s and 1930s.

KICKSHAWS

Kimball was originally called Antelopeville.

Kimball County once was the site of America's largest U.S. Air Force Intercontinental Ballistic Missile underground silo launch installations.

The Overland Trail passed through the county.

THE COURTHOUSE
WAS ADDED TO THE
NATIONAL REGISTER OF
HISTORIC PLACES IN 1990.

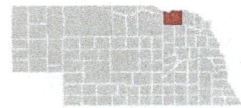

KNOX COUNTY

COUNTY SEAT: CENTER • LICENSE PLATE PREFIX: 12 • POPULATION: 8,298
GOVERNED BY SEVEN COUNTY SUPERVISORS

The Knox County Courthouse dates to 1934 with support from the Civilian Works Administration (CWA) and the Federal Emergency Relief Administration (FERA). It has had two additions over the years.

The county was established by the Nebraska Territorial Legislature in 1857 as L'Eau Qui Court, the Ponca name for the Niobrara River. By 1873, the county was reorganized and renamed in honor of Maj. Gen. Henry Knox, secretary of war under George Washington.

The courthouse includes three accessible levels and two annexes. The lower level houses the sheriff's office and jail.

The middle level contains offices for elected officials, their vaults, the DMV and the zoning administrator.

The upper level features the district courtroom, jury room and offices of the judge and clerk, the offices of the public defender and probation officer, plus the county court and clerk's offices and the county attorney's office.

The austere building is well-organized for county business. A new commissioners' meeting room is notably spacious. The county clerk's office features two old ballot boxes and a yesteryear poster showcasing one-room schoolhouses in the county's 30 townships.

The north annex houses the Nebraska Extension and the highway superintendent, while the south annex is home to offices for Health and Human Services, Veterans Services, the economic development director and emergency management services.

KICKSHAWS

The county borders South Dakota to the north and is adjacent to the Missouri River, with nine protected recreational areas.

The 2014 addition was funded by inheritance tax funds.

PRISONERS MADE BRICKS FOR THE ORIGINAL 1934 COURTHOUSE.

LANCASTER COUNTY

COUNTY SEAT: LINCOLN • LICENSE PLATE PREFIX: ORIGINALLY 2; NOW ALPHA-NUMERIC
POPULATION: 326,716 • GOVERNED BY FIVE COUNTY COMMISSIONERS

On a gray day in early March 2023, I was fortunate to check in with the Lancaster County Administrator's Office and meet two county commissioners.

Lancaster County, established in 1859 and named after Lancaster, England, is home to a modern office building designed by Lincoln architects Clark & Enersen and Hemphill, Berg & Dawson. Completed in 1967, the building has underwent a major remodel in 1998 and the addition of the Justice Law Enforcement Center in 2000.

The integration of city and county governments reduces service duplication and streamlines operations. Joint departments include property management, planning, purchasing, human resources and some communications functions, including a local TV station, LNK TV.

The first floor is dedicated to the county's elected officials, county commissioners and the county/city chambers. It also features public art and an art gallery. City finance and city council offices are located on this floor as well.

The Justice Law Enforcement Center, which houses the sheriff, county attorney and the clerk of the district court, is an integral part of the complex.

The building's second and third floors, accessible by elevator or a grand stairway, are home to various city departments and officials, including the mayor and the mayor's conference room.

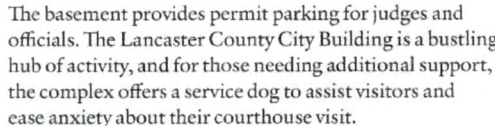

The basement provides permit parking for judges and officials. The Lancaster County City Building is a bustling hub of activity, and for those needing additional support, the complex offers a service dog to assist visitors and ease anxiety about their courthouse visit.

KICKSHAWS

Before the Social Security System, 53 counties in Nebraska operated poor farms or county homes for the indigent. In 1920, these facilities provided shelter and basic care to 452 paupers. The Lancaster County Poor Farm, established in the late 19th century, closed in 1962.

Lancaster County employs 901 people and operates a large juvenile detention center and a mental health crisis center serving Region V. The county also has a jail, built in 2013, with capacity for 786 inmates.

SPANNING TWO CITY BLOCKS, THE COUNTY COMPLEX HOUSES A RANGE OF FUNCTIONS, INCLUDING CITY OFFICES, MOST COUNTY OFFICES AND VARIOUS COURTS, INCLUDING ONE FOCUSING ON MENTAL HEALTH.

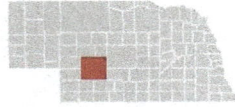

LINCOLN COUNTY

COUNTY SEAT: NORTH PLATTE • LICENSE PLATE PREFIX: 15 • POPULATION: 34,676
GOVERNED BY FIVE COUNTY COMMISSIONERS

The Lincoln County Courthouse embodies a rich historical legacy that began in 1860 when the area was first designated as Shorter County and there was considerable hostility between the Sioux and Cheyenne Indians and the federal government along the Platte River Valley.

In 1866, when the county was reorganized, the name was changed to honor Abraham Lincoln, the nation's 16th president who had been assassinated the previous year.

In 1867, the county seat was moved from Cottonwood Springs to North Platte. The county's present boundaries were established in 1871, and its first courthouse was built in 1874 and destroyed by arson in the early 1920s – while the present courthouse was being built.

The arsonist, the county treasurer, was embezzling money and feared being discovered. So he attempted to burn down the courthouse to cover his tracks. Unfortunately for him, the courthouse records survived the blaze.

The current courthouse, designed by George A. Berlinghof and Cecil Calvert Coursey, was completed the following year. It gained an addition in 1968 and was listed on the National Register of Historic Places in 1990.

The Beaux-Arts/Classical Revival design was among the costliest courthouses built in Nebraska and the longest under construction, spanning a decade due to a shortage of funds. It was 1932 before the building was complete.

The building features gray marble wainscoting, intricately tiled flooring, golden oak woodwork and frosted glass transoms. The main floor features a pair of tiled murals, one featuring a covered wagon and a buffalo; the other, a locomotive and a market steer.

The hallways feature historical artifacts, photos and a pair of tiled wall murals depicting the progress of the county, from covered wagons and buffalo to locomotives and cattle. A whimsical touch is a cutout of President Lincoln that occupies an office chair when the office holder is away.

KICKSHAWS

The North Platte Canteen was a vital stop for World War II troop trains passing through the state.

The county covers an area of 2,564 square miles and ranks among the top seven beef cow counties in the U.S.

THE DISTRICT COURTROOM IS ONE OF THE LARGEST IN NEBRASKA WITH GALLERY SEATING FOR 150.

Buffalo Bill State Historical Park honors the legacy of Buffalo Bill Cody, a showman and prominent figure of the American West. The park is located on the outskirts of North Platte, where Cody once had a ranch.

LOGAN COUNTY

COUNTY SEAT: STAPLETON • LICENSE PLATE PREFIX: 87 • POPULATION: 655
GOVERNED BY THREE COUNTY SUPERVISORS

I timed my visit to Stapleton for an overnight stay at The Bunkhouse B&B on Main Street. The next morning, I headed to the Logan County Courthouse, arriving right as it opened at 8 a.m.

The original courthouse – a one-time hotel – was destroyed by fire in 1962, and a new building was constructed the following year.

Stapleton wasn't always the county seat. When Logan County's boundaries were finalized by the Nebraska Legislature in 1885, the village of Gandy held that designation. The county seat moved to Stapleton in 1930 – the last county seat change in Nebraska's history.

The county is named after Gen. John A. Logan, a soldier and politician who played a key role in establishing Memorial Day, honoring those who sacrificed their lives in service to the nation. The county's early settlers were predominantly Civil War veterans.

Entering the courthouse, county officials' offices and vaults are located on the right side of the main hallway, while the county's sizable library occupies the left side. The supervisors have a dedicated meeting room (with a fainting couch!) and a new county shop building at a nearby location.

In smaller rural counties like this one with a limited number of employees (24), roles overlap out of necessity. Thus, the clerk and treasurer handle a variety of responsibilities here. The day of my visit, the DMV office had been closed for a month due to staffing issues.

The courtroom in this well-maintained building is bright and airy, with light wood finishes.

The facility not only is a key employer in the county but also reflects a commitment to local norms, closing all county offices over the noon hour.

KICKSHAWS

Logan County is part of the North Platte Micropolitan Statistical Area.

Most of the state's courthouses accommodate the Nebraska Extension through interlocal agreements.

HISTORICALLY, 20 PERCENT OF NEBRASKA'S EARLY COURTHOUSES WERE DESTROYED BY FIRE.

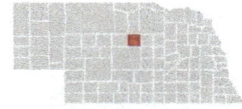

LOUP COUNTY

COUNTY SEAT: TAYLOR • LICENSE PLATE PREFIX: 88 • POPULATION: 592
GOVERNED BY THREE COUNTY COMMISSIONERS

I visited the Loup County Courthouse in Taylor after a relaxing Memorial Day weekend at Uncle Buck's Lodge in neighboring Brewster.

The county, established by the Nebraska Legislature in 1883, derives its name from the North Loup River that meanders through the region.

Taylor is the county's sole incorporated town. The courthouse, a modest white frame building, is situated across the street from the city park.

The courthouse is a simple, one-story, fireproof structure built in 1957. The interior is functional and straightforward, furnished with older, utilitarian furniture. The courtroom is small and unadorned, with metal folding chairs in the gallery.

Despite its simple appearance, the courthouse is well-organized, clean and effectively meets the needs of its citizens, reflecting Loup County's practical approach to administration.

And just for fun, "Taylor Villagers," life-sized plywood cutouts of historical figures, dot the village.

KICKSHAWS

In 1940, the Loup County Sheriff was killed while attempting to serve a warrant. The suspects were later apprehended and convicted.

The county is home to the ornamental Taylor Cypress tree, also known as the Taylor Juniper.

The county has one unsolved murder. In June 2000, near Almeria, an unincorporated area west of Taylor, a rancher was shot six times in his bed.

THE LOUP COUNTY HISTORICAL SOCIETY BUILDINGS ARE LOCATED ONE BLOCK NORTH OF THE COURTHOUSE.

MADISON COUNTY

COUNTY SEAT: MADISON • LICENSE PLATE PREFIX: 7 • POPULATION: 35,627
GOVERNED BY THREE COUNTY COMMISSIONERS

Madison County, established in 1867, has uncertain origins. The county is either named after President James Madison or reflects the early settlers' ties to Madison, Wisconsin. What is certain is that the area's early history includes notable visits from the Lewis and Clark Expedition and surveyors of the Louisiana Territory.

Originally, Norfolk was the designated county seat. However, after years of contention, a decisive election shifted the county seat to Madison by majority vote.

The current courthouse, designed by Everett J. Simpson, was completed in 1977. It is a modern, single-story building situated along a circular drive on a spacious lot, giving it a campus-like feel.

The interior features a central commons area with a skylight, surrounded by county offices on the perimeter. The building is wheelchair accessible and includes modern, tidy offices with vaults and safes. The floorplan includes a large DMV office and driver's exam area, county and district courts, offices for court personnel, a jury room, a law library and access to the sheriff's office and jail facility.

The courthouse is equipped with contemporary furniture and displays a typical array of photos, maps and the county flag. The courtrooms are modern and tastefully designed, featuring wood accents and trim alongside a portrait gallery of former judges.

KICKSHAWS

In 1920, women won the right to vote and soon were represented on juries in Nebraska.

The original jail is used as office space. The new jail, built in 1999, has 120 beds.

THIS AGRICULTURAL AREA HAD NO SIZABLE POPULATION UNTIL THE ARRIVAL OF THE RAILROADS.

McPHERSON COUNTY

COUNTY SEAT: TRYON • LICENSE PLATE PREFIX: 90 • POPULATION: 383
GOVERNED BY THREE COUNTY COMMISSIONERS

McPherson County, established in 1890 and named after Civil War Gen. James B. McPherson, initially had a courthouse made of sod, known throughout the Plains as a "soddy," which served Tryon for many years. This was later replaced by a one-story brick courthouse that was destroyed by a tornado in 2003.

The county's current courthouse, its third, was completed in 2005. Inside this compact yet efficient facility, elected officials often juggle multiple roles for practical reasons. The structure is fully accessible, fireproof and well-organized, with documents securely stored in office vaults.

Amid the typical array of yesteryear photos, maps and art are several Charles Russell prints of the American West. The courtroom is handsome, complemented by a meeting room that doubles as a jury room and a sheriff's office. The furnishings throughout are contemporary and practical, designed to meet the needs of a small yet vital county.

KICKSHAWS

The county had 150 residents some 80 years ago when Mrs. Jay Smith famously declared, "Let's keep tryin' (Tryon) to have a town."

 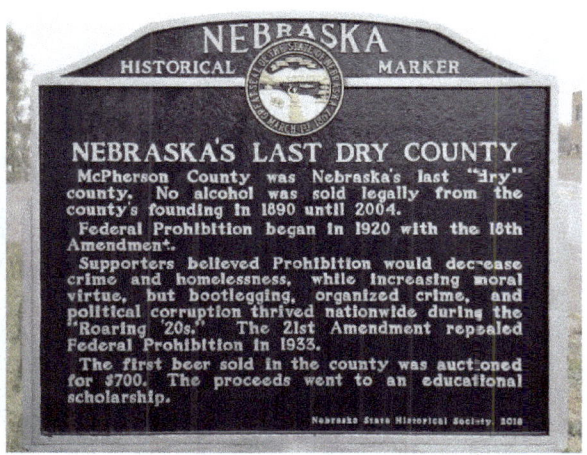

McPHERSON COUNTY IS THE LEAST-POPULOUS COUNTY IN NEBRASKA,
FOLLOWED BY ARTHUR AND BLAINE.

MERRICK COUNTY

COUNTY SEAT: CENTRAL CITY • LICENSE PLATE PREFIX: 46 • POPULATION: 7,755
GOVERNED BY SEVEN COUNTY SUPERVISORS

The Merrick County Courthouse in Central City has deep roots in Nebraska.

Established in 1858, the county is named in honor of Elvira Merrick, wife of the speaker of the House of Representatives in the Nebraska Territorial Legislature.

Built in 1915 and designed by William F. Gernandt in the Classical Revival style, the courthouse underwent a significant expansion in 2007 to house the County Justice Center, a notable enhancement.

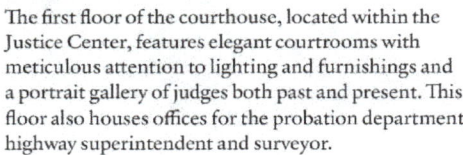

The first floor of the courthouse, located within the Justice Center, features elegant courtrooms with meticulous attention to lighting and furnishings and a portrait gallery of judges both past and present. This floor also houses offices for the probation department, highway superintendent and surveyor.

The second level of the original section includes spaces for the DMV, planning and zoning departments, assessor, clerk, register of deeds, election commissioner, treasurer and document storage vaults.

The sheriff, county attorney, Veterans Services and supervisors operate from the third floor.

A few original furnishings are preserved, including a writing desk and a plat table. Architectural highlights include original office doors and marble-tread stairs with iron railings.

KICKSHAWS

The county's triangular shape is defined by its southern boundary along the Platte River.

MERRICK COUNTY IS NEBRASKA'S ONLY COUNTY NAMED FOR A WOMAN.

MORRILL COUNTY

COUNTY SEAT: BRIDGEPORT • LICENSE PLATE PREFIX: 64 • POPULATION: 4,504
GOVERNED BY THREE COUNTY COMMISSIONERS

Morrill County was established in 1909 after a petition from residents on the northern edge of Cheyenne County who sought its division. Named in honor of Charles H. Morrill, president of the Lincoln Land Company, the county is situated in the Mountain Time Zone.

The Mormon, Oregon and Black Hills Trails, as well as the Pony Express route, passed through the region, serving as crucial routes for pioneers, settlers and mail carriers in the 19th century.

The courthouse, a Classical Revival-style building designed by J.P. Eisentraut of Kansas City, was completed in 1910. In 1998, an annex was added to accommodate the growing needs of the county. This modern, fireproof addition provides office and vault space for the clerk, treasurer and assessor. It also houses the surveyor, Veterans Services and DMV.

A sweeping staircase, marble floors and period woodwork contributed to this western Nebraska jewel's addition to the National Register of Historic Places in 1990.

The annex features a diverse array of displays, including a unique map of Nebraska where each county is marked by its license plate prefix. The exhibits also showcase Ducks Unlimited prints and vibrant renderings of Courthouse Rock, Jail Rock and Chimney Rock, among other geographical landmarks in the Panhandle.

On the first level of the original courthouse, you'll find county court probation services and the commissioners' meeting room. The second level houses the district courtroom, jury room and law library.

KICKSHAWS

In 1865, the area that is now Morrill County was the site of the Battle of Mud Springs, fought between the U.S. Army and a coalition of Cheyenne, Lakota, Sioux and Arapaho warriors. The conflict was part of the larger Indian Wars, as both sides struggled for control and survival.

In 1949 and 1950, oil and gas were discovered in Morrill County.

In the 2010 primary election for sheriff of Morrill County, a tie between candidates was broken by drawing cards.

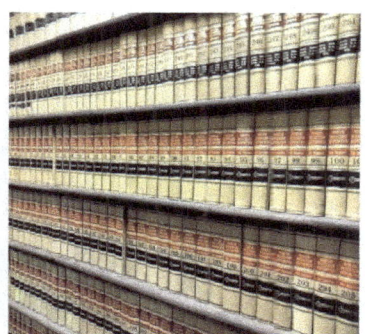

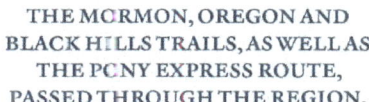

THE MORMON, OREGON AND BLACK HILLS TRAILS, AS WELL AS THE PONY EXPRESS ROUTE, PASSED THROUGH THE REGION.

NANCE COUNTY

COUNTY SEAT: FULLERTON • LICENSE PLATE PREFIX: 58 • POPULATION: 3,274
GOVERNED BY SEVEN COUNTY SUPERVISORS

I was taken aback to discover a mountain lion inside the Nance County Courthouse – specifically, a taxidermy display donated by a private party. Positioned near the front door, this unique feature provides visitors with an intriguingly memorable welcome and selfie opportunity.

Established in 1879, Nance County was named after Albinus Nance, Nebraska's youngest governor who was just 30 years old when elected.

The area's history is rich and varied: the Pawnee Nation lived here for centuries before settlers arrived.

As the Mormons pushed through the prairie in the years before statehood, conflicts with the Sioux and Pawnee Tribes, blizzards, famine, disease and a prairie fire took their toll.

Fullerton was founded by Randall Fuller, who organized expeditions from Wisconsin to the California gold fields between 1849 and 1860. During his many trips across Nebraska, he developed an affection for the Fullerton area. In 1876, he relocated there with his family to raise cattle; a year later, he platted the town.

The original courthouse was replaced in 1976 with a modern one-story brick building designed by architect George E. Clayton. This new courthouse was constructed in front of the original, which was then demolished. In 2023, the courthouse received significant updates, including courtroom improvements, accessibility enhancements and technological upgrades.

KICKSHAWS

Timber and lush grasses were major assets of early Nance County.

Fullerton hosted the largest Chautauqua in Nebraska and "the best one between Omaha and Denver" between 1912 and 1920.

For a period, Nebraska Wesleyan University was in Fullerton before moving to Lincoln.

THE LOUP RIVER FLOWS THROUGH THE COUNTY, STRETCHING FROM WEST TO EAST.

Nebraska's golf history is traced to April 4, 1887, when Scottish-American course designer Alexander Findlay and his childhood friend, Edward C. Millar, played six holes on Millar's Merichiston Ranch near Fullerton. As far as anyone can document, it was one of the first rounds of golf played in the United States.

NEMAHA COUNTY

COUNTY SEAT: AUBURN • LICENSE PLATE PREFIX: 44 • POPULATION: 7,076
GOVERNED BY THREE COUNTY COMMISSIONERS

Nemaha County, established in 1855 by the Nebraska Territorial Legislature, takes its name from a creek associated with the Otoe Tribe.

Initially, the county seat was Brownville, but after several elections, Auburn became the central hub.

The courthouse, located in the southern part of town, has been welcoming visitors since 1900. Designed by Lincoln architect George A. Berlinghof and built with local stone, the structure embodies the Classic style of the early 20th century.

Its layout features a basement jail, a first floor dedicated to the offices of county officials and their vaults and a second floor for the district court. Accessibility is ensured with a chair glide.

The building is impeccably maintained, featuring period-appropriate doors, woodwork and furniture. The interior is distinguished by attractive tile floors, a grand stairway, wainscoting and steam heat radiators. The old safes, still in use, are a touchstone to the past.

Recent updates include remodeled windows and modernized air conditioning and courtroom facilities. The day of my visit, exterior work was underway, with ongoing improvements to the foundation, landscaping and sidewalks.

KICKSHAWS

The county has a flood plain administrator.

Brownville, 10 miles east of Auburn, offers a glimpse into its 1854 origins. Nearby Peru is home to Nebraska's first state college.

Nemaha County is home to Indian Cave State Park, a notable destination with both natural beauty and historical significance.

Worth a visit: While in Auburn, stop by the post office to see the 1930s mural by Ethel Magafan.

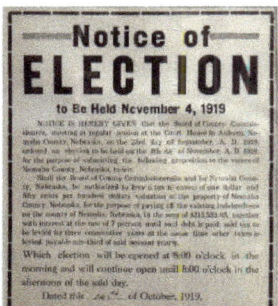

NUCKOLLS COUNTY

COUNTY SEAT: NELSON • LICENSE PLATE PREFIX: 42 • POPULATION: 4,095
GOVERNED BY THREE COUNTY SUPERVISORS

The Nuckolls County Courthouse stands as a distinguished landmark in a county established in 1871.

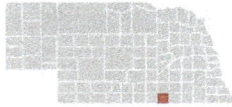

Spanning 24 square miles, the county honors Stephen F. Nuckolls, who was instrumental in its creation and significantly contributed to the formation of seven other counties in southeastern Nebraska, as well as the founding of Nebraska City. A native of Virginia, Nuckolls was among the early settlers of the Nebraska Territory and a slave owner.

The Neoclassical courthouse was designed by George E. McDonald and constructed in 1890.

The building's two-story stucco exterior and its well-preserved interior offer a glimpse into late 19th-century design, updated with wood paneling in 1990.

The main floor is home to the offices of the assessor, clerk, treasurer, road department and drivers' license examiner. On the top floor, you'll find the courtroom with handsome wood accents, a law library and jury room, plus offices of the clerk of the district court, county attorney and county judge.

The building features accessible amenities, including a lift for second-floor access. Important documents are stored in safes and vaults, including a distinctive two-story vault for the clerk of the district court. Carpeted floors in some areas and handsome wood furnishings enhance the functional environment. The building, however, lacks a sprinkler system.

The sheriff's office is located in a nearby building.

KICKSHAWS

If a courthouse has a tower, you can bet there are bats in the belfry. Nebraska Supreme Court Administrator Corey Steel recalls bats interrupting district court proceedings in Nuckolls County to the degree that former Gov. Ben Nelson got involved. He threatened the suspension of court cases until the bell tower was sealed and the bats removed. A similar situation had to be addressed in Hamilton County.

OTOE COUNTY

COUNTY SEAT: NEBRASKA CITY • LICENSE PLATE PREFIX: 11 • POPULATION: 16,335
GOVERNED BY FIVE COUNTY COMMISSIONERS

On a brisk winter morning, I headed to Nebraska City for a tour of the Otoe County Courthouse with the county commission chair. Established in 1855, Otoe County has maintained its seat in Nebraska City, honoring its namesake, the Otoe Tribe.

Designed by architect A.G. Basset in a striking Georgian style that echoes early American colonial architecture, the courthouse features a distinctive red brick facade. Opened in 1864, it proudly stands as the oldest courthouse in Nebraska still in active use.

The courthouse has been updated numerous times but remains well-preserved. The basement, mostly used for storage, has some original jail cells that are open for tours.

On the main floor is a large mural by Frank Zimmerer, commissioned in 1952. It depicts Nebraska City, from the Iowa side of the Missouri River. Zimmerer also painted the circa 1955 mural in the district courtroom of the Cuming County Courthouse in West Point.

The main floor is a hub of county business, featuring offices and meeting rooms for elected officials, with modern vaults for document preservation. The district court offices and jury room are on the second floor.

The county preserves its history through old photos, maps, displays and furnishings. Highlights include the original service counters in the clerk's office, a bell rope and an antique fire hose in a circular rack. Amid the historic touches, the courthouse features new windows, updated light fixtures and modernized courtrooms. Otoe County was among the first in the state to adopt a paperless system, equipping commissioners with tablets to streamline county operations.

KICKSHAWS

William "Bill" Sutherland was in custody on a murder charge on August 11, 1891, when an angry mob forcibly removed him from the courthouse jail and hanged him from a nearby railroad bridge.

Several founding families of Nebraska City, including J. Sterling Morton, owned slaves. Morton was a two-time governor, U.S. secretary of agriculture under Grover Cleveland and founder of Arbor Day. Historic Arbor Day Lodge, built in 1882, was his summer residence.

OTOE COUNTY BOASTS 27 REGISTERED HISTORIC PLACES.

PAWNEE COUNTY

COUNTY SEAT: PAWNEE CITY • LICENSE PLATE PREFIX: 54 • POPULATION: 2,512
GOVERNED BY THREE COUNTY COMMISSIONERS

I am unlikely to forget my May 12, 2023, trip to Pawnee City. Returning to Lincoln, I was pursued by a tornado for 40 miles.

The Pawnee County Courthouse, established in 1854 and named after the Pawnee Tribe, is the historic centerpiece of the county.

Constructed in 1911 and designed by architect William F. Gernandt in the Classical Revival style, the courthouse features a distinctive limestone and brick façade and basement access via a formal porch on the north side. Recent additions, such as a veterans memorial courtyard at the entrance, further enhance the courthouse's presence on the square.

Inside, you'll find decorative tile flooring, iron railings with ornate newel posts and elegant marble wainscoting.

The basement accommodates the county commissioners' meeting room, Veterans Services, Nebraska Extension, and a meeting room that doubles as a driver's exam area.

The second floor houses the offices of elected officials, including the assessor, clerk, treasurer, county judge and county court. This floor also features original service counters and displays a collection of historical paintings, prints, photos, maps, antique clocks, signage and period furnishings. Many doors and some of the woodwork and light fixtures are original to the building.

The third floor is dedicated to the district court offices and a law library. The courtroom is utilitarian with wooden theater-style chairs with wire hat racks beneath the seats. A balcony, previously part of the courtroom, was removed several years ago following a fire marshal's request.

This floor also features the judge's quarters, jury room, probation office and the sheriff's office. Originally, the courthouse's top floor housed the jail, with the sheriff and his family living on-site and providing meals for prisoners.

KICKSHAWS

Pawnee County has experienced a decline in population over the past 20 years.

The county has six wildlife management areas and shares its southern border with Kansas.

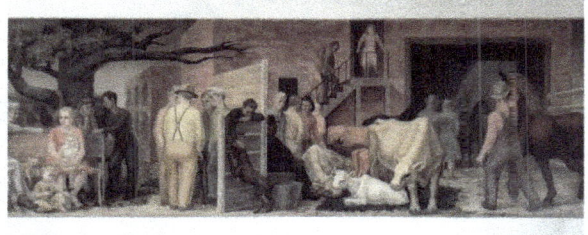

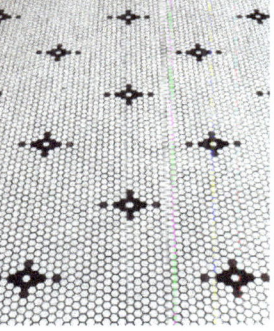

PERKINS COUNTY

COUNTY SEAT: GRANT • LICENSE PLATE PREFIX: 74 • POPULATION: 2,795
GOVERNED BY THREE COUNTY COMMISSIONERS

Perkins County is home to a distinguished example of a 1920s courthouse on the Plains. Designed by J.F. Reynolds of Sioux City, Iowa, in the Classical Revival style, the 1927 building has been thoughtfully updated and meticulously maintained.

During my visit, funding for HVAC upgrades was a topic of conversation, highlighting the ongoing challenges of preserving an historic structure.

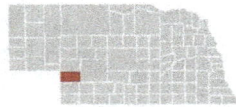

Established in 1887, Perkins County was created from the southern half of Keith County, stretching to the Colorado border. It was named in honor of Charles E. Perkins, president of the Burlington, Chicago and Quincy Railroad.

Grant, the eventual county seat, emerged victorious from a competition with three other villages, despite allegations of ballot-box tampering. The town's status was cemented with the arrival of the first train on July 4, 1887.

The ground floor of the courthouse features offices for Veterans Services, emergency management and the highway and weed departments. Access to the second level is provided by a recently installed elevator and a grand staircase with decorative black iron railings and gray-veined marble wainscoting.

The second floor houses offices for elected officials and document storage vaults, including what is believed to be the largest clerk's vault in the state. The terrazzo hallways are handsomely decorated with benches, clocks, a county flag, prints, photos, maps, barn art, signs and framed blueprints of the courthouse.

The third floor features the county court office, courtroom and jury room, emergency management and sheriff's office.

KICKSHAWS

Perkins County is in the Mountain Time Zone.

The first settlers arrived in 1885.

THE UPDATED DISTRICT COURTROOM MAINTAINS OLD-TIME CHARM IN ITS GALLERY BENCH SEATING, LIGHT FIXTURES AND CROWN MOULDING, PILASTERS AND FOCAL WALL BEHIND THE JUDGE'S BENCH.

PHELPS COUNTY

COUNTY SEAT: HOLDREGE • LICENSE PLATE PREFIX: 37 • POPULATION: 9,057
GOVERNED BY SEVEN COUNTY COMMISSIONERS

The Phelps County Courthouse is a notable example of early 20th-century architecture. Designed by William F. Gernandt in the Classical style, it was completed in 1911 and is the third courthouse in the county's history.

The county was established by the Nebraska Legislature in 1873 and named after William Phelps – a widely known steamboat captain and trader. The courthouse, which has undergone several modifications, is complemented by a modern County Justice Center completed in 2004. An elevator ensures accessibility.

The first floor holds offices for emergency management, zoning, Health and Human Services and Veterans Services. The symmetrical grand staircase, central to the interior design, features striking white marble with black and gray veining and decorative black cast iron railings and newel posts. Marble wainscoting and a gracefully curved landing contribute to the staircase's grandeur.

The second floor is home to the treasurer, motor vehicle department, clerk, assessor, probation officers and county supervisors. The Justice Center, located in the addition, houses the offices of the sheriff, state patrol and CASA.

The third floor houses the county judge's office, the clerk of the district court, the district judge's office, the district courtroom, jury room and law library. There also are safes and vaults for document preservation.

The district courtroom retains its early 20th-century aesthetic, with decorative wood wainscoting, gallery seats with ornate iron supports and hardwood swivel chairs in the jury box. Tall windows and doors with transoms add historic character, while an arched alcove with a statue of Lady Justice creates a focal point for the bench.

Throughout the courthouse, halls are adorned with maps, photos, western art prints, signage and the county flag. The atmosphere is welcoming and the staff is friendly.

KICKSHAWS

Holdrege is served by an Amtrak station.

There was a large World War II POW camp in Atlanta, within the county.

In the 1860s, pioneers from Sweden settled in the area.

PIERCE COUNTY

COUNTY SEAT: PIERCE • LICENSE PLATE PREFIX: 40 • POPULATION: 7,299
GOVERNED BY THREE COUNTY COMMISSIONERS

Pierce County was established in 1859 by the Nebraska Legislature and named in honor of Franklin Pierce, the 14th president of the United States.

The county seat has consistently been Pierce. Historically, the area was significant to the Ponca Tribe as rich hunting and fishing grounds.

The original red brick courthouse, built in 1889, served the community until the mid-1970s. The current two-story brick building, completed in 1978, stands on the same site, with the old structure having been razed.

Designed by architect Everett J. Simpson, the modern facility accommodates not only county government offices but also the jail and spaces for economic development, zoning and Nebraska Extension.

The clerk's office provided a guided tour down spacious, long, carpeted halls with modern signage and typical courthouse elements like maps, posters, displays, photos, prints and calendars.

Each office, including those of elected officials, incorporates vaults for document storage, ensuring both accessibility and security.

The building is designed to be fireproof and particular attention has been given to creating accessible service counters in the clerk, treasurer and assessor areas. Another notable feature is an exercise room for employee wellness.

The midcentury modern courtrooms are spacious, with honey colored woodwork. The county is part of the Norfolk Micropolitan Statistical Area.

KICKSHAWS

Originally, Pierce County contained 15 townships and a "dog leg" in its otherwise straight northern boundary with Cedar County. On February 5, 1875, Cedar County awoke to discover that the Nebraska Legislature had amputated its "jog" and designated it as Pierce County. The adopted township has been known as "Dog Town" ever since.

This poster print of Lady Justice is popularly displayed in courthouses across Nebraska. The illustration is by Beth Stover of the National Women's Law Center.

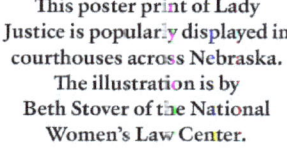

PLATTE COUNTY

COUNTY SEAT: COLUMBUS • LICENSE PLATE PREFIX: 10 • POPULATION: 34,609
GOVERNED BY SEVEN COUNTY SUPERVISORS

Platte County traces its origins to 1855 when Dodge County was divided into three parts: Dodge, Colfax and Platte. The county was formally organized in 1856 under a commissioner system with three elected officials and takes its name from the French word for "flat." The courthouse, designed by Platte County native Charles Wurdeman of Columbus, Nebraska, was constructed in 1922. An annex was added in 1977. Enhancements for accessibility included an elevator.

The original building is designed in the Neoclassical Revival style, characterized by an emphasis on symmetry and simplicity. More restrained than its Beaux-Arts cousin, the interior maintains an austere elegance with its preference for unadorned walls. Notable features include gray-veined Italian marble wainscoting, honeycomb-tiled flooring with geometric detailing and ornate crown moulding. Original light fixtures, antique benches and a pair of mounted buffalo heads create a striking contrast against the white walls and gray-painted wood trim that complement the marble's rich veining.

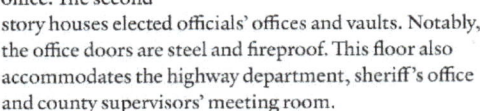

The raised basement is home to the emergency management office. The second story houses elected officials' offices and vaults. Notably, the office doors are steel and fireproof. This floor also accommodates the highway department, sheriff's office and county supervisors' meeting room.

The former county district court courtroom on the third floor has been divided into office space but the upper part retains the outline of the courtroom, including its decorative moulding and a mural of Lady Justice.

The annex contains the county and district courtrooms and associated offices, jury room, law library, adult diversion program office and driver's license exam room. The courtrooms are bright and spacious, decorated with framed portraits of previous judges.

KICKSHAWS

Columbus was one of the first areas to populate when Nebraska became a territory.

In the winter of 1867, a mob breached the jail and hung Bob Wilson, an alleged murderer, on a now-gone cottonwood tree at the corner of 7th Street and 22nd Avenue.

THE COURTHOUSE WAS ADDED TO THE NATIONAL REGISTER OF HISTORIC PLACES IN 1990.

POLK COUNTY

COUNTY SEAT: OSCEOLA • LICENSE PLATE PREFIX: 41 • POPULATION: 5,228
GOVERNED BY THREE COUNTY COMMISSIONERS

The Nebraska Legislature first established Polk County in 1856 but didn't finalize its boundaries until 1873. The county's namesake, James K. Polk, was the 11th president of the United States.

In the early days, county records were kept in the homes of elected officials in the absence of a courthouse. A small frame courthouse was eventually erected in Osceola, but it was destroyed by fire in 1881, resulting in the loss of many important documents.

The second courthouse, a brick structure, served the county until the current Beaux-Arts building – a grand citadel with a hilltop perch – was completed in 1922. Designed by William F. Gernandt, the courthouse features elegant terra-cotta trim and fireproof steel doors on the record rooms and vaults.

The courthouse interior is visually striking with its marble floors, stairs, wainscoting and trim. Although the building is not fully accessible, staff are prepared to assist visitors on the first floor. Notably, Polk County has 17 offices and departments, including one providing Senior Services.

On the first floor, visitors will find the driver's license examiner (available on Tuesdays), Nebraska Extension, highway superintendent, planning and zoning, surveyor, Veterans Services and weed supervisor. The second floor houses the elected officials, Aging Partners and emergency management offices.

The third floor is home to the clerk's offices for both county and district courts, the county attorney's office, judges' chambers, courtroom, probation office, jury room and law library. The old jail is now used for storage and the judge's office area still contains remnants of an apartment utilized when judges traveled from county to county.

The courtroom is particularly handsome with its spacious design, fine woodwork, period light fixtures, ceiling beams and novel cork tile flooring. Although wheelchair access is limited to the first floor, the building's rich historical and architectural significance makes it a worthwhile visit.

KICKSHAWS

The northern boundary of Polk County is the Platte River.

The courthouse's impressive view from Nebraska Highway 92 establishes it as a distinguished landmark.

THE HALLS ARE ADORNED WITH PERIOD FURNISHINGS, INCLUDING BENCHES, CLOCKS, MAPS, PHOTOS, RADIATORS, AN OLD FILING SYSTEM AND VARIOUS SIGNS AND POSTERS.

RED WILLOW COUNTY

COUNTY SEAT: McCOOK • LICENSE PLATE PREFIX: 48 • POPULATION: 10,457
GOVERNED BY THREE COUNTY COMMISSIONERS

I made my first trip ever to McCook in July 2023. What a beautiful Nebraska town!

The Red Willow County Courthouse on Norris Avenue opened its doors in 1927. Designed by Marcus L. Evans, the building reflects the architectural elegance of its time and was extensively remodeled and updated in 1993.

Red Willow County was established in 1873 and named after a creek that meanders through the area. Early disputes over the county seat and where records would be kept eventually were settled, with McCook winning the honors.

A spacious marble lobby sets the tone for the building's grandeur. This elegant entryway features a row of vintage green metal mailboxes, a prominent "In God We Trust" wall stencil, and the offices of elected officials, each with secure vaults (one with a vintage stack flat file and reading table).

The architectural elements throughout are impressive, with curving ceiling treatments, capitals and pillars. I was particularly captivated by a trio of stained-glass windows in the stairway. Marble floors, well-maintained throughout, add to the building's elegance.

The upper level houses the district courtroom, along with offices for court personnel, a jury room and a law library. The courtroom boasts unique woodwork, including distinctive trim, a prominent bench and rounded dark wood pediments above the windows and doors, creating an impressive and dignified atmosphere.

KICKSHAWS

In 2014, McCook added a new law enforcement center and correctional facility with 30 beds.

The community is served by an Amtrak station, with the California Zephyr running between Chicago and Emeryville, California.

The Republican River flows through part of the county.

The southern edge of Red Willow County borders the northern edge of Kansas.

IN THE COUNTY, 10 LOCATIONS ARE LISTED ON THE NATIONAL REGISTER OF HISTORIC PLACES, INCLUDING THE COURTHOUSE AND THE GEORGE NORRIS HOUSE.

RICHARDSON COUNTY

COUNTY SEAT: FALLS CITY • LICENSE PLATE PREFIX: 19 • POPULATION: 7,689
GOVERNED BY THREE COUNTY COMMISSIONERS

Established in 1854 and reorganized the following year by the first territorial legislature, Richardson County was named in honor of William A. Richardson of Illinois, the third territorial governor of Nebraska. The county seat has always been Falls City, where, over the years, three courthouses have been built on the same site.

The current Classical Revival courthouse, designed by William F. Gernandt, was constructed between 1922 and 1925 and officially opened its doors in 1925.

The courthouse sits on an open square, a contrast to tree-lined surroundings noted in historic renderings. Inside, visitors are greeted by lots of marble, decorative tile and numerous tributes to veterans, including a museum.

The lower level accommodates the Nebraska Extension, Health and Human Services, DMV, highway engineer and emergency management and operations personnel. The first floor houses the treasurer, Veterans Services and the War Museum. The second floor features offices for elected officials, the county court, probation services and SENCA (a community action agency).

The third floor, often considered the jewel of Nebraska courtrooms, houses the district courtroom and its associated offices, jury room and law library.

The courtroom is a remarkable space, with 10-foot walnut wood panels rising behind the bench. Vaulted ceilings are adorned with stained glass and indirect lighting in shades of green and pink.

The nearby sheriff's office and jail add to the courthouse's significant presence in the community.

KICKSHAWS

Richardson County is the eastern most county in Nebraska. It falls within the emergency planning zone (EPZ) for the Cooper Nuclear Station in Brownville, Nemaha County.

Falls City is known as the "City of Art" and is home to the John Falter Museum celebrating the work of the prominent American illustrator and artist.

In 1857, the area served as a base on the Lane Trail, a key route from Iowa used by free-state emigrants to bypass pro-slavery Missouri enroute to Kansas.

OVER THE YEARS, THE COUNTY HAS BEEN A STATE LEADER IN HOG, COAL AND OIL PRODUCTION.

Two prominent murals enhance the courtroom: "The Explorer Meeting With Indians" behind the judge's bench and "Pony Express Rider" at the rear of the chamber. This courtroom has been the site of notable trials, including the Rulo murders and the Teena Brandon cases, and has also appeared in films including "Boys Don't Cry."

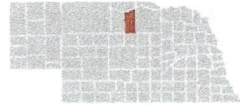

ROCK COUNTY

COUNTY SEAT: BASSETT • LICENSE PLATE PREFIX: 81 • POPULATION: 1,271
GOVERNED BY THREE COUNTY COMMISSIONERS

The Rock County Courthouse is steeped in local history and notable for its distinctive architectural style.

Rock County was established in 1888, carved from Brown County by popular vote and named for its rocky terrain. The first courthouse, a frame building constructed in 1889, was destroyed by fire. A replacement was built on the same foundation in 1897, closely following the original plans. This structure was later razed to make way for the current courthouse, completed in 1940 with WPA funds.

Designed by E.B. Watson in the Art Deco style, this landmark was added to the National Register of Historic Places in 1990.

The first two levels of the building are dedicated to various county offices, including that of the sheriff. These offices are equipped with vaults and safes to ensure document security. Circular steel stairs – a frequently seen courthouse feature – provide access to additional storage on the lower level.

The courthouse has terrazzo floors and marble stairs. The building is not accessible, so those with mobility issues may find it challenging to navigate.

The walls and hallways are adorned with the typical variety of local artifacts and decorations, including posters, maps, artwork and a Military Honor Roll. Noteworthy are a county-themed pieced quilt and a large mural depicting the courthouse's three iterations.

The third floor houses the district courtroom, a spacious area featuring oak woodwork and 1940s furnishings, including theater-style gallery chairs. The oak bar, bench and jury box are all part of the original design. A chair rail wraps the room, defining the federal blue paint on the lower wall section.

The upper floor also includes offices for the judge and court personnel, as well as a jury room.

KICKSHAWS

William Albert "Kid" Wade, 21, was hung in Bassett in 1884 for stealing horses and the payroll at Fort Niobrara. He was strung up on a railroad whistle post by area vigilantes, who called themselves The Regulators.

Bassett is home to one of Nebraska's largest livestock auction companies.

The county is known for its twin lakes and the Niobrara River on its northern border.

NEW DEAL FUNDING, INCLUDING THE WPA, ASSISTED IN BUILDING AND REMODELING 11 OF NEBRASKA'S COURTHOUSES.

SALINE COUNTY

COUNTY SEAT: WILBER • LICENSE PLATE PREFIX: 22 • POPULATION: 14,555
GOVERNED BY FIVE COUNTY COMMISSIONERS

The Saline County Courthouse is a pride point for the Czech Capital of Nebraska. The county, established by the Nebraska Territorial Legislature in 1855 and organized in 1867, was named for the salt deposits once believed to be in the area. Wilber has served as the county seat since 1877.

The five-story courthouse was built in 1926-1927, following the demolition of an 1878 building on the same site. The architect, Marcus L. Evans of Hastings, also designed the courthouse in Red Willow County. Built in the Classical Revival style from Bedford limestone, it was the pinnacle of modern design at the time.

In 2019, the County Citadel underwent significant expansions and updates and is now fully accessible and equipped with metal doors and vaults.

The marble used on staircases, railings, mopboards and wainscoting is in sleek contrast to the ornate plasterwork of columns, cornices and capitals and dark woodwork. The hallways are intentionally sparse, but have period light fixtures, built-in water fountains and benches.

The lower level houses emergency management offices, while the first floor includes offices for the clerk of the county court, probation, Veterans Services and DMV, plus an assembly room. Elected officials and the county roads department have offices on the second floor.

The third floor is dedicated to the district courtroom and its associated offices, including a jury room. The formal courtroom is one of the most remarkable in Nebraska, with original hanging fixtures, high ceilings with painted crown mouldings, extensive walnut paneling and cork flooring. The finishing touch: arched urn pediments crowning the doors.

The fourth floor holds the county attorney's offices, while the new law enforcement center addition houses the sheriff's office, Nebraska Extension and Aging Services.

KICKSHAWS

The railroad arrived in Wilber in 1871, contributing to its growth and connectivity.

The Saline County Courthouse joined the National Register of Historic Places in 1990.

Some offices feature art, including two paintings by the renowned Czech artist Tobias.

SEVERAL HIGH-PROFILE COURT CASES HAVE APPEARED ON THE DOCKETS, INCLUDING THE AUBRY TRAIL AND BAILEY BOSWELL MURDER AND DISMEMBERMENT OF SYDNEY LOOFE IN 2017.

Saline County saw one of the state's more bitter and prolonged county seat fights, dating from the 1870s and rekindled in 1920. Efforts to build the present courthouse began in 1920 and created seven years of conflict between Crete and Wilber.

SARPY COUNTY

COUNTY SEAT: PAPILLION • LICENSE PLATE PREFIX: ORIGINALLY 59, NOW ALPHA-NUMERIC
POPULATION: 199,886 • GOVERNED BY FIVE COUNTY COMMISSIONERS

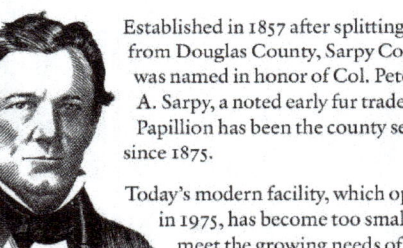

Established in 1857 after splitting from Douglas County, Sarpy County was named in honor of Col. Peter A. Sarpy, a noted early fur trader. Papillion has been the county seat since 1875.

Today's modern facility, which opened in 1975, has become too small to meet the growing needs of the county. As a result, county business has expanded to include five additional buildings scattered around Papillion.

The courthouse, accessed via Golden Gate Drive, houses essential county functions, including offices and vaults for elected officials, a large auditorium and eight courtrooms – four county courts, one mental health court and four district courts.

Discussions are ongoing about a new courthouse to better meet current needs and future growth. Meanwhile, adjacent to the courthouse, the county correctional center was surrounded by construction activities, reflecting ongoing efforts to improve that facility.

The courthouse itself resembles a modern office building, with expansive windows and clean, functional design. The courtrooms are well-appointed with contemporary furnishings.

For visitors, the courthouse offers helpful amenities, including displays, art and historical information just inside the west entrance. The building is equipped to handle a diverse population, with services available in multiple languages and interpreters on hand.

The county, which has 743 employees, has an independent election commissioner's office responsible for managing and overseeing electoral processes.

KICKSHAWS

By 1860, Sarpy County had a population of 1,201, while Lancaster County had a population of just 153.

Explorers Lewis and Clark camped near the Missouri River bordering Bellevue and the Sarpy County area in 1804.

The first Nebraska newspaper, the Nebraska Palladium, was launched in 1854 in Bellevue, today Sarpy County's largest city.

SARPY COUNTY IS THE SMALLEST COUNTY BY AREA (241 SQUARE MILES) AND THE THIRD-LARGEST COUNTY BY POPULATION IN NEBRASKA.

SAUNDERS COUNTY

COUNTY SEAT: WAHOO • LICENSE PLATE PREFIX: 6 • POPULATION: 23,463
GOVERNED BY SEVEN COUNTY COMMISSIONERS

It was snowing when I ventured to Wahoo from Lincoln for a tour of the Saunders County Courthouse, a hilltop landmark since 1904.

Saunders County, originally named Calhoun when it was created in 1856, was renamed in 1862 to honor Alvin Saunders, a U.S. senator from Nebraska and the final and longest-serving governor of the Nebraska Territory.

The Otoe and Pawnee Tribes lived and camped in the region before the first settlement, Ashland, became the county seat in 1867. In 1873, following an election, the county seat was moved to Wahoo, where a two-story frame courthouse was built. The building was later destroyed by fire.

The current courthouse, designed by Omaha architects Fisher & Lawrie, is a striking example of early 20th-century Italian Renaissance Revival architecture.

Completed in 1904, this brick and terra-cotta structure made a notable impression with its modern amenities, including electricity and steam heat, and exquisite finishing touches. Highlights include fleur-de-lis mosaic-tiled floors; stained glass, plaster, wood and brass ornamentation, and stencils and murals relating to agriculture and pioneer life.

Particularly noteworthy are the county supervisors' meeting room on the second floor and the district courtroom on the top floor. The meeting room has stained-glass doors, stenciled ceilings and intricate plaster details. The district courtroom boasts rich walnut paneling, gilt-edged plaster on the ceiling, detailed woodwork around the witness and jury boxes and a commanding arched mural of Justitia with two attendants behind the bench.

This courthouse truly is a "Palace on the Plains."

KICKSHAWS

The county has three wildlife management areas and two state recreation areas.

Saunders County is bordered on the north and east by the Platte River.

The Saunders County Museum is located one block south of the courthouse.

SCOTTS BLUFF COUNTY

COUNTY SEAT: GERING • LICENSE PLATE PREFIX: 21 • POPULATION: 35,699
GOVERNED BY FIVE COUNTY COMMISSIONERS

Scotts Bluff County was formed in 1888 from a larger Cheyenne County, taking its name from the Scotts Bluff landmark in the Platte Valley and fur trapper Hiram Scott, who died near it. Gering won the county seat designation in 1889 after a contentious election with Mitchell.

The present courthouse, designed by William N. Bowman of Denver in 1920, is a fine example of Classical Revival architecture, notable for its imposing columns and stately presence. It sits on a campus that includes the Scotts Bluff County Administrative Offices, completed in 1978.

Upon entering the courthouse, visitors pass through security and are welcomed by an impressive three-story atrium. The interior boasts elegant tile floors, marble stairs, wainscoting and original woodwork, complemented by period ironwork, signage, clocks and benches.

The courthouse has four county courtrooms and a district courtroom. The county courtrooms are smaller and have been updated for modern use, ensuring efficiency.

In contrast, the district courtroom retains a traditional ambiance with dark wood paneling, a large wood panel behind the bench and a photo gallery of past judges. A sizable balcony is no longer accessible to the public.

The administrative office building is fully accessible and has an open, airy design enhanced by natural light. The building houses various county departments and is decorated with flags, art, displays, maps and plants.

The lower level of the administrative building holds emergency management, a communication center and Veterans Services. The first floor is home to elected officials' offices and the DMV. The second floor includes the sheriff's office, probation services, the health department and the county commissioners' meeting room.

KICKSHAWS

The county is home to the Scotts Bluff National Monument, a prominent geological landmark along the Oregon Trail. Gering was founded at the base of the bluff in 1887.

The North Platte River flows through a part of the county, which shares it western boundary with Wyoming.

The county has the third busiest airport in Nebraska.

THE OREGON, CALIFORNIA, PONY EXPRESS AND MORMON TRAILS ALL PASSED THROUGH THE COUNTY.

THE HISTORIC COURTHOUSE AND THE MODERN ADMINISTRATIVE OFFICES ARE SITUATED ON THE EASTERN SIDE OF THE BLUFFS, OFFERING EXCELLENT PHOTO OPPORTUNITIES OF THE LANDSCAPE.

SEWARD COUNTY

COUNTY SEAT: SEWARD • LICENSE PLATE PREFIX: 16 • POPULATION: 17,671
GOVERNED BY FIVE COUNTY COMMISSIONERS

Seward County was originally established in 1855 and formally organized in 1867 as Greene County, in honor of Colton Greene, a Missouri businessman and soldier.

However, Greene's association with the Confederacy was unpopular in Civil War-era Nebraska Territory, where anti-secession sentiments were strong. As a result, the county was renamed Seward County in 1862, in tribute to William H. Seward, Abraham Lincoln's secretary of state.

Seward's founders, Lewis and Mary Moffitt, played a crucial role in the town's establishment by donating the land and contributing additional funds from their estate for the courthouse. The gift, coupled with a bond issue, enabled construction of George Berlinghof's design. Renowned for courthouse designs across Nebraska, Kansas and Iowa, he provided Seward with a striking example of Classical Revival architecture.

The old frame courthouse burned. County offices operated out of a second-floor space in a building on North Seward Street for years.

Completed in 1904, the replacement courthouse's construction exceeded budget, which delayed the building of the accompanying jail. Berlinghof's design reflects his vision of a county capitol. In 2023, government operations were spread across three buildings in downtown Seward: the courthouse on Seward Street, the Justice Center built in 2016 on 8th Street, and the West Wing on 14th Street.

KICKSHAWS

Pittsburgh, in Seward County, was founded in 1873 at a location once believed to be rich in peat. However, the town was abandoned by 1875. It is suspected that the postmaster may have mistakenly recorded the town's name as Pittsburgh instead of the intended Peatsburg.

The Big Blue River flows through the county, which is part of the Lincoln Metropolitan Statistical Area.

Seward County has three wildlife management areas and two waterfowl production areas.

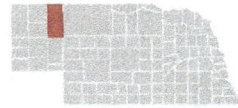

SHERIDAN COUNTY

COUNTY SEAT: RUSHVILLE • LICENSE PLATE PREFIX: 61 • POPULATION: 4,928
GOVERNED BY THREE COUNTY COMMISSIONERS

Freshly fallen snow made for a picturesque visit to the Sheridan County Courthouse in Rushville.

Established in 1885 from a portion of Sioux County, Sheridan County was named in honor of Union Army Gen. Philip H. Sheridan, a cavalry leader assigned to Nebraska following the Civil War.

The selection of Rushville as the county seat was a dramatic affair. Initially, Hay Springs was chosen through what many believed was electoral fraud. This led to a legal battle culminating in 1888 when the Nebraska Supreme Court declared Rushville the official county seat.

The courthouse itself, a striking red brick structure completed in 1904, stands as a monument to that pivotal decision. Designed by W.T. Misner of Omaha, the building's cornerstone was laid by the Masonic Order.

Local artifacts and period accents are highlights of the interior, including mosaic tile floors, woodwork and Daniel Long Soldier prints of Native American culture.

The main floor accommodates various elected officials, many of whom juggle multiple roles. This floor houses essential facilities, including vaults for record preservation, a meeting room for the commissioners and a driver's licensing office that is open one day a week.

The second level, accessible via a chair glide, is dedicated to judicial functions. It includes the district courtroom, its associated offices, a law library and a jury room. The courtroom itself is relatively plain, with limed oak paneling on the bench and a collection of judge portraits lining the walls. The furnishings are a mix of period pieces, including theater-style seats with wire hat racks.

KICKSHAWS

North of Hay Springs, there's an unusual cliff formation known as Beaver Wall. The county also has Sandoz, a village named for Jules Sandoz, the father of acclaimed Nebraska novelist Mari Sandoz.

The unincorporated village of White Clay had a reputation for exacerbating alcoholism on the nearby Pine Ridge Reservation. In 2017, the Nebraska Liquor Control Commission made a significant change by denying liquor licenses to businesses in the village, effectively mitigating the problem.

THE SOUTHERN PART OF THE COUNTY HAS EXPANSIVE RANGELAND; THE NORTHERN PART, PINE-COVERED HILLS. GORDON IS THE LARGEST CITY WITH A POPULATION OF 1,612.

SHERIDAN COUNTY IS 2,440 SQUARE MILES, MAKING IT THE FOURTH LARGEST COUNTY IN NEBRASKA.

SHERMAN COUNTY

COUNTY SEAT: LOUP CITY • LICENSE PLATE PREFIX: 56 • POPULATION: 2,983
GOVERNED BY THREE COUNTY COMMISSIONERS

A weekend stay in the Sand Hills included a stop in Loup City for a tour of the Sherman County Courthouse.

Sherman County, established by the Nebraska Legislature in 1871 and organized in 1873, was named for Gen. William Tecumseh Sherman, a Civil War hero who commanded cavalries in Nebraska and neighboring states. Loup City was chosen as the county seat the same year.

The courthouse, designed by Henningson Engineering Co., is a three-story tan brick building with terra-cotta trim. Its design reflects the grandeur of the Beaux-Arts style, with classical detailing and an imposing presence.

The interior boasts original tile floors, marble stairs, doors and woodwork. Recent updates have included replacement of the windows. Access remains a challenge due to the absence of an elevator.

The lower level houses the sheriff's office, DMV and Nebraska Extension. The main floor holds elected officials' offices, commissioners' meeting room, county attorney's office, weed department and child support services.

Throughout the courthouse are original service counters, furnishings and benches. The building's halls and offices are adorned with historical elements such as two Regulator clocks, photos, maps, ballot boxes, signs and flags.

The top floor houses the county court and district court, complete with their respective offices, a jury room and a vault. The district courtroom stands out for its dark wood ceiling beams, gallery benches and stained glass windows.

KICKSHAWS

Soon after the county was organized, the initial crops were devasted by grasshoppers, posing a severe challenge to early settlers. Additionally, the county experienced numerous cattle raids by Native American tribes as the buffalo herds, which had once been a primary food source, dwindled.

On Flag Day 1934, a riot occurred on the courthouse grounds, sparked by a march led by Mother Bloor, a Chicago-based labor organizer attempting to organize farmers and ranchers in Nebraska. Tensions between the marchers and locals escalated, resulting in fines and jail sentences for the instigators.

APPROXIMATELY ONE-THIRD OF RESIDENTS OF THE COUNTY ARE OF POLISH-AMERICAN DESCENT.

SHERMAN RESERVOIR STATE RECREATION AREA IS ONE OF THE COUNTY'S BIGGEST ATTRACTIONS.

SIOUX COUNTY

COUNTY SEAT: HARRISON • LICENSE PLATE PREFIX: 80 • POPULATION: 1,154
GOVERNED BY THREE COUNTY COMMISSIONERS

Harrison serves as the county seat and is also now the only incorporated town in Sioux County. The county, named for the native Sioux Tribe living in the area, was created in 1857 after having been attached to Cheyenne County for 20 years. The boundaries were finalized in 1877 and redefined in 1885. An election chose Harrison as the county seat.

The courthouse, constructed in 1931, reflects the Classical Revival style as designed by the E.L. Goldsmith Co. The two-story building, notable for its Italian marble floors, stairs and trim, remains without air conditioning.

The first floor houses county offices, including those for the sheriff and Nebraska Extension. There also is a community meeting room and dedicated office space for the village of Harrison.

The offices feature furnishings and light fixtures from the 1930s. The walls are decorated with photos, maps, western art and flags, while the ceilings boast dark wood mouldings.

The district courtroom is located on the second floor, which also includes the judge's office, jury room and law library. The landing area is highlighted by a large stained-glass window. The courtroom features traditional elements: medium-sized bench, two-tier jury box with foot rests and bench seating for the gallery. Photos of previous judges adorn the walls.

KICKSHAWS

Sioux County's western border is shared with Wyoming. Also, the county is situated within the Oglala National Grasslands, a vast expanse of protected prairie.

Worth a visit: Fort Robinson Museum & History Center near Crawford and Agate Fossil Beds National Monument near Harrison.

HARRISON HAS THE HIGHEST ELEVATION OF ANY TOWN OR COUNTY SEAT IN NEBRASKA, AT 4,876 FEET.

STANTON COUNTY

COUNTY SEAT: STANTON • LICENSE PLATE PREFIX: 53 • POPULATION: 5,856
GOVERNED BY THREE COUNTY COMMISSIONERS

Stanton County has an interesting history behind its name. Initially, it was established in 1856 as Izard County, after Mark W. Izard, Nebraska's territorial governor at the time. In 1862, the name was changed to honor Edwin M. Stanton, President Abraham Lincoln's secretary of war. Stanton County was organized three years later.

The current courthouse, a one-level brick structure built in 1976, replaced its predecessor on the same site.

Designed by architect Everitt J. Simpson, the building reflects a modern design in housing 16 county offices, with the central portion accommodating the offices of the clerk, treasurer and assessor, including their vaults.

The west wing is home to Veterans Services, commissioners, planning and zoning personnel and the driver's license examiner. The east wing contains the sheriff's office and the county and district courtrooms.

A notable feature is the life-sized cutout honoring three hometown soldiers who lost their lives in Mideast conflicts. Additionally, a clock in the clerk's office is from the old courthouse, dating to 1876.

The courtroom in the east wing is modern and tastefully appointed, with the bench and bar featuring contrasting dark woodwork.

KICKSHAWS

There are 3,144 county courthouses across the United States.

The county and its Elkhorn River attracted settlers of German, Norweigan, Czech, Irish, Canadian and Swedish origin.

When the Fremont, Elkhorn and Missouri Valley Railroad was built in 1879, the pioneers here had new marketing outlets for their grain and livestock.

THE ELKHORN RIVER FLOWS THROUGH THE UPPER PORTION OF THE COUNTY.

THAYER COUNTY

COUNTY SEAT: HEBRON • LICENSE PLATE PREFIX: 32 • POPULATION: 4,829
GOVERNED BY THREE COUNTY COMMISSIONERS

Thayer County was established under different names in 1856 and was officially renamed in 1871 to honor John M. Thayer, a pioneer settler and governor of Nebraska from 1887 to 1892. Hebron was designated the county seat, a decision contested by other villages for 25 years.

The original courthouse, built on donated land in Hebron, was a two-story frame structure that burned in July 1900, with only the documents in the vaults surviving. A new courthouse was constructed in 1902. Designed by George Berlinghof in the Classical-Gothic style, it featured Indiana Bedford stone and bore strong resemblance to his design for the Nemaha County Courthouse in Auburn.

After damage from a 1953 tornado, the county removed the clock tower, corners, gables, minarets and spires, leaving a more streamlined roofline.

The building is accessible and features marble floors, stairs, wainscoting and trim. The lower level houses Veterans Services, Health and Human Services, Nebraska Extension and a community meeting room.

The second level contains offices for elected officials, their vaults and the commissioners' boardroom. The staircase features decorative white iron railings and newel posts, complemented by columns and decorative capitals. The space has original woodwork, doors and marble counters, etched glass signage and period furnishings.

The top level of the courthouse is home to the district courtroom and a law library, along with the offices of the clerk of the district court, zoning, emergency management and probation. The courtroom is spacious with bench seating, and wood paneling highlights the judge's bench and jury box. Dark wood moulding, columns and painted decorative capitals add a dignified touch.

KICKSHAWS

Only two courthouses in Nebraska are known to have been struck by tornadoes: Thayer and McPherson. McPherson's courthouse had to be rebuilt.

Thayer County was a notable center for the Nebraska Women's Suffrage movement, with significant activities taking place here, starting in 1879.

THE STONEWORK ABOVE THE COURTHOUSE'S EAST ENTRANCE REMAINS A MYSTERY.
MANY BELIEVE IT WAS CREATED BY GUTZON BORGLUM, THE SCULPTOR OF MOUNT RUSHMORE.

MANY HISTORIC TRAILS PASSED THROUGH THAYER COUNTY, INCLUDING THE OREGON TRAIL,
THE CALIFORNIA TRAIL, THE PONY EXPRESS ROUTE AND THE OVERLAND STAGECOACH ROUTE.

THOMAS COUNTY

COUNTY SEAT: THEDFORD • LICENSE PLATE PREFIX: 89 • POPULATION: 677
GOVERNED BY THREE COUNTY COMMISSIONERS

I paired a visit to the Thomas County Courthouse in Thedford with a visit to the Cherry County Courthouse in Valentine. Along the way, I picked up a speeding ticket on U.S. Highway 83!

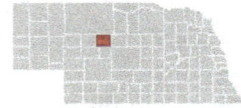

Thedford has served as the county seat since 1887, when Thomas County was established by the legislature and named in honor of Civil War hero Gen. George H. Thomas.

The county's development was significantly influenced by landmark legislation, including the Preemption Act of 1841, the Homestead Act of 1862, the Timber Culture Act of 1873 and the Kinkaid Act of 1904, all of which encouraged settlement in the Sand Hills.

The most pivotal force in the county's growth and prosperity, however, was the Burlington Railroad.

When the original courthouse was destroyed by fire in the early 1920s, other towns made attempts to claim the county seat. Thedford remained steadfast, conducting county business from a temporary wood-frame building until a replacement could be built.

That courthouse served the county until it was replaced in 2006 by a modern one-story building, financed through inheritance funds and a loan. The arched window in the entrance pays homage to the design of the original courthouse. The floor plan consolidates all county offices and the Nebraska Extension under one roof.

The spaces are well-maintained and bright, with clear signage and original artwork on loan from the Thedford Art Gallery. The district courtroom is outfitted with handsome, understated maple chairs and benches with vertical back slats, creating a pristine and orderly look.

KICKSHAWS

Local lore tells of a cattle thief who was lynched with barbed wire after being taken from jail.

Before the county was organized, the area was open range. Cattlemen drove their herds north from Texas to sell beef to the U.S. government to feed American Indians on reservations in South Dakota. Without landmarks, however, the shifting waves of sand confused more than one party in the early days.

IN ADDITION TO LARGE CATTLE RANCHES, THOMAS COUNTY BOASTS THE NEBRASKA NATIONAL FOREST LOCATED NEAR HALSEY BETWEEN THE MIDDLE LOUP AND DISMAL RIVERS.

A bronze sculpture on the courthouse grounds honors the Haumann sisters, Retta, 4, and Tillie, 8, who became lost in the Sand Hills in 1891 while returning home from a neighbor's house. Retta was found alive some 25 miles away; Tillie's body was discovered 75 miles from home.

THURSTON COUNTY

COUNTY SEAT: PENDER • LICENSE PLATE PREFIX: 55 • POPULATION: 6,557
GOVERNED BY SEVEN COUNTY SUPERVISORS

Thurston County was originally established as Blackbird County in 1855, in honor of Omaha Chief Blackbird. The name was changed to Thurston County in 1889 to recognize U.S. Sen. John M. Thurston, following the county's reorganization and the designation of Pender as the county seat.

Pender's first courthouse was an eight-room schoolhouse built in 1895, repurposed for county use. The building faced several remodeling challenges, including conversion of the basement into a jail. In 2009, to address the need for modernization and accessibility, an addition with an elevator was constructed on the west side of the building.

The first floor serves as the elevator lobby, with new carpeting and preserved classroom doors. The walls are showcases for maps, photos, paintings and prints.

The second level houses offices for the assessor, sheriff, clerk, treasurer, Veterans Services, maintenance and communications, plus vaults for record preservation.

The third level is dedicated to judicial functions. The courtroom, shared by county and district courts, features the judge's bench at front, jury box to the right and spectator benches down the center.

Adjacent rooms include the jury room and offices for the judge, county attorney, county court and clerk of the district court. The vault is located here, too, along with the county boardroom and law library.

A recent addition has notably enhanced the courthouse's functionality and accessibility.

KICKSHAWS

The legend of the county is that Omaha Chief Blackbird had a favorite campsite on a hill overlooking the Missouri River on the county's eastern border. When he died in 1800, it is said he was buried there seated on his horse. Lewis and Clark visited his grave in 1804.

In the late 1800s and early 1900s, settlers of German heritage began arriving in the area. Today, Omaha and Ho-Chunk reservations encompass the county's entire land area of 396 square miles.

FIFTY-TWO PERCENT OF THE COUNTY'S POPULATION IS NATIVE AMERICAN. AMONG ITS CELEBRATED FIGURES IS DR. SUSAN LA FLESCHE PICOTTE, THE FIRST AMERICAN INDIAN WOMAN TO BECOME A PHYSICIAN IN 1889. HER SISTER, SUSETTE LA FLESCHE TIBBLES, ALSO KNOWN AS BRIGHT EYES, WAS PONCA CHIEF STANDING BEAR'S INTERPRETER DURING HIS 1879 TRIAL AT FORT OMAHA.

VALLEY COUNTY

COUNTY SEAT: ORD • LICENSE PLATE PREFIX: 47 • POPULATION: 4,012

GOVERNED BY SEVEN COUNTY SUPERVISORS

On May 26, 2023, we visited the Valley County Courthouse in Ord on our way to Uncle Buck's Lodge in Brewster for the weekend.

Valley County, established in 1871 and organized two years later, derives its name from the picturesque valley nestled between the North and Middle Loup rivers.

Ord, the county seat, has been home to three courthouses. The current Beaux-Arts structure has been in use since 1921. Located on Courthouse Square, this three-story gem was designed by William F. Gernandt.

The interior makes an impression with grand public spaces dressed in white, dark gray and black marble, from classical geometric tiled floors, to imposing staircases, newel posts, wainscoting and trim.

The lower level houses a community room, the DMV office, jail and sheriff's office. In total, Valley County operates 16 offices and departments within this space.

The second floor is dedicated to the county's elected officials and their vaults, with notable features such as a stained-glass door for the boardroom. The walls are adorned with a rich assortment of maps, prints, historical photographs and informative displays. Of particular interest is the treasurer's collection of courthouse memorabilia and antique license plates.

The highlight is the district courtroom on the top floor. This grand space is distinguished by its extensive wood paneling, formal door trim, coffered ceiling and central skylight. The remainder of this floor includes court offices, jury room and law library.

For those visiting Ord, checking in with the clerk of the district court is a must to fully appreciate the grandeur of the district courtroom.

KICKSHAWS

In North Loup, Popcorn Days is Nebraska's longest-running community celebration.

In 2010, a dam broke in Valley County, causing significant damage in the village of North Loup.

Evelyn Sharp, an early 20th-century aviator born in Ord, is honored with the Evelyn Sharp Airfield.

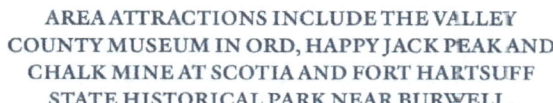

AREA ATTRACTIONS INCLUDE THE VALLEY COUNTY MUSEUM IN ORD, HAPPY JACK PEAK AND CHALK MINE AT SCOTIA AND FORT HARTSUFF STATE HISTORICAL PARK NEAR BURWELL.

In the early 2000s, the Valley County auditor discovered that the county treasurer, who had served for several years, had been misappropriating funds and falsifying records. This led to a high-profile investigation and legal action.

WASHINGTON COUNTY

COUNTY SEAT: BLAIR • LICENSE PLATE PREFIX: 29 • POPULATION: 21,152
GOVERNED BY SEVEN COUNTY SUPERVISORS

Washington County was one of the eight original counties established in the Nebraska Territory in 1854, with boundaries ratified in 1855 and revised in 1860. Named in honor of the nation's first president, George Washington, the county saw its seat move from Fort Calhoun to Blair in 1869.

The courthouse complex, nestled on Colfax Street in a residential area south of Blair's business district, includes the original 1891 brick courthouse – a three-story structure crowned with a tower. Designed by architect O.H. Placey, the building has seen several upgrades, including significant improvements by the WPA in 1936.

A southern annex houses spacious offices for various elected officials and fireproof vaults.

The more recent northern annex accommodates law enforcement, the sheriff's office and the jail.

The original courthouse's primary function is home of the district court.

The ground floor houses the emergency management office. (Given the proximity of the Omaha Public Power District's deactivating Fort Calhoun nuclear plant, the area is equipped with a 10-mile Emergency Planning Zone and evacuation routes.)

On the second floor, visitors will find the offices of the clerk of the district court, the county attorney and the county court, all housed in a building where historic fireplaces have been preserved.

The third floor's district courtroom is a traditional space adorned with elegant wood trim, a handsome judge's bench and jury box and bench seating for spectators. The room is surrounded by historical photographs, adding to the courtroom's rich atmosphere.

KICKSHAWS

Washington County is home to Fort Atkinson State Historical Park at Fort Calhoun. The 1850s fort sat hundreds of miles from the nearest civilian settlement on the American frontier.

Worth a visit: DeSoto National Wildlife Refuge east of Blair, where you can see the reclaimed steamboat Bertrand that sank in 1865 in the Missouri River on the eastern boundary of the county.

GEORGE WASHINGTON'S FIRST JOB AT AGE 17 WAS AS A SURVEYOR IN VIRGINIA.
HE WAS HIRED BY LORD FAIRFAX TO MAP OUT COUNTY LINES AND ESTABLISH COUNTY SEATS.

WAYNE COUNTY

COUNTY SEAT: WAYNE • **LICENSE PLATE PREFIX: 27** • **POPULATION: 9,874**
GOVERNED BY THREE COUNTY COMMISSIONERS

Wayne County was established by gubernatorial proclamation in 1870 and officially defined by legislative action in 1871 in honor of Revolutionary War Gen. "Mad" Anthony Wayne. Initially, the county seat was in Taffee, later moving to La Porte before settling in Wayne following a decisive election in 1882.

The first courthouse, a frame building, was destroyed by fire on July 4, 1884. The current courthouse, an impressive Richardsonian Romanesque designed by Orff & Guilbert of Minneapolis, was completed in December 1899.

Situated north of Wayne's business district, in a serene residential area, the courthouse is a striking and beautiful landmark. A prominent veterans memorial in front adds to its commanding presence. The courthouse is accessible and has been meticulously maintained, including a significant renovation project completed in 2002.

The lower level includes the Nebraska Extension, driver's examination area (open every Wednesday) and a variety of displays, including a Military Honor Roll and elevator access.

On the main floor, you'll find the offices of county roads, assessor, treasurer and clerk, each with its vault. This level is adorned with paintings, prints, historical photos, maps, a clock, signs, quilts and a framed 1923 U.S. flag.

The second floor is home to the commissioners' meeting room, the district courtroom, county court office, clerk of the district court and Veterans Services. The courtroom maintains a traditional aesthetic with decorative wood trim and a panel behind the judge's bench with the carved inscription: Justice. The jury box and bar are well-crafted and the spectator seating, equipped with wire hat racks, is reminiscent of a theater. The room is spacious and bright, yet maintains a somber tone fitting of its purpose.

A final stop north of the courthouse took me to a building housing the sheriff's office and emergency management.

KICKSHAWS

Both previous county seat villages are no longer in existence because the railroad eventually shifted its route to Wayne.

The county is home to Wayne State College, established in 1891, and the Sioux Strip State Wildlife Management Area.

THE COURTHOUSE STANDS ON DONATED LAND ATOP A HILL, PROMPTING THE LOCAL NEWSPAPER OF THE TIME TO APTLY CALL IT THE "CASTLE IN THE CORNFIELDS."

The floors feature decorative tile, while the oak woodwork, including doors, trim and stairs, adds a touch of elegance.

WEBSTER COUNTY

COUNTY SEAT: RED CLOUD • LICENSE PLATE PREFIX: 45 • POPULATION: 3,351
GOVERNED BY FIVE COUNTY COMMISSIONERS

Webster County was established in 1867 and organized in 1871. It's named in honor of U.S. Sen. Daniel Webster of Massachusetts, counted among the greatest orators, statesmen and political powers of his day.

The arrival of the Burlington and Missouri River Railway in 1879 accelerated Red Cloud's growth as the county seat.

The present-day courthouse, the county's second, is a brick structure completed in 1914 and designed by William F. Gernandt in the Second Renaissance Revival style. It stands proudly on courthouse square, north of the main street, in a quiet residential neighborhood.

Red Cloud is renowned for its literary connection to Willa Cather, and the courthouse plays a role in her works. The building evokes a nostalgic atmosphere with its wooden floors, historic maps, 19th-century prints and photos lining the walls. The period light fixtures, iron stair rails and newel posts further enhance its old-time charm.

Spaces are furnished with classic pieces, though there are modern amenities such as an elevator. However, the building lacks a sprinkler system. Behind the courthouse stands Nebraska's oldest jail, operational since 1877. Plans for a new facility are currently in discussion.

The first floor houses several offices, including the Nebraska Extension, highway department, weed control and South Heartland Health Department. The second floor is dedicated to the county's elected officials, with offices for the assessor, treasurer and clerk, and additional spaces for Veterans Services and driver's license exams. Notable on this floor are the circular steel stairs leading to storage areas below.

The third floor is home to the county court, county attorney and magistrate offices. The courtroom is straightforward, with a raised wooden bench, a well-crafted jury box and a bar. Spectators are seated on simple metal chairs. This floor also contains an extensive law library and a photo gallery of past judges.

KICKSHAWS

In 1910, the county's population was 12,008.

Worth a visit: The National Willa Cather Center, the author's childhood home in Red Cloud, the Willa Cather Foundation and the Willa Cather National Prairie.

THE REPUBLICAN RIVER FLOWS THROUGH THE SOUTHERN PART OF THE COUNTY, WHILE THE SOUTHERN BOUNDARY ABUTS KANSAS.

WHEELER COUNTY

COUNTY SEAT: BARTLETT • LICENSE PLATE PREFIX: 84 • POPULATION: 775
GOVERNED BY THREE COUNTY COMMISSIONERS

A significant attraction in Bartlett is the largest outdoor bronze sculpture garden in the Midwest, located immediately north of the current courthouse and extending onto the lawn of the old courthouse.

On display are 42 sculptures by native son Herb Mignery, a member of the Cowboy Artists of America Hall of Fame. Mignery, of Loveland, Colorado, grew up on a ranch near Bartlett and spent 50 years sculpting Western Americana.

Wheeler County, established by the legislature in 1877 and named after Daniel Wheeler, long-serving secretary of the Nebraska State Board of Agriculture, was not formally organized until 1881. Bartlett emerged as the county seat and successfully retained that status despite challenges.

The current courthouse, a modest building erected in 1982, replaced the old courthouse, which had been condemned by the fire marshal. The single story six-room facility is designed to be fireproof. It houses the county's two full-time elected officials, who manage a variety of responsibilities typical in smaller counties, and their staffs.

The modest courtroom and judge's office appear new, largely due to their limited use. The courtroom, in fact, is primarily used as meeting space for the county commissioners.

KICKSHAWS

The area saw an influx of settlers after the passage of the 1904 Kinkaid Act.

While in Bartlett, check out the Wheeler County Museum, housed in the old county courthouse. For recreation, visit Pibel Lake.

"MY LEGACY WILL PROBABLY BE A SCULPTURE GARDEN IN A LITTLE TOWN IN THE MIDDLE OF NEBRASKA AND I'M MORE THAN SATISFIED WITH THAT."
— HERB MIGNERY, IN A 2020 INTERVIEW WITH NEBRASKA PUBLIC MEDIA

YORK COUNTY

COUNTY SEAT: YORK • LICENSE PLATE PREFIX: 17 • POPULATION: 14,356
GOVERNED BY FIVE COUNTY COMMISSIONERS

Established in 1855 and officially organized in 1870, York County pays tribute to the House of York, in honor of the founders of the capital of Yorkshire, England, and the American settlers with English ancestry who came to the area.

The courthouse, situated in downtown York, was constructed in 1980, replacing a much-admired structure known as the "Palace on the Plains," which was demolished in 1978.

The modern courthouse, designed by Berggren Architects, underwent a significant remodeling project in 2020. The renovation focused on updating the dispatch office and creating a new entrance for the sheriff's office.

The courthouse, spanning three levels, boasts a functional and contemporary design with warm tones, spacious halls and minimal clutter. A notable feature in the entry is an inlaid tile design reminiscent of a barn quilt.

The lower level houses a meeting and training room and offices for emergency management, investigations and maintenance.

The first level is dedicated to the offices and vaults of the elected officials. This floor includes the offices of the clerk, register of deeds, assessor, treasurer, DMV, voter registration and Veterans Services. The commissioners' boardroom also is here. The furnishings throughout this level are modern and functional.

The top floor is home to various legal and administrative offices, including CASA, the county attorney, court systems, child support services and the public defender.

The building is fully accessible, with an elevator to all floors.

KICKSHAWS

The area saw an influx of settlers after the passage of the 1904 Kinkaid Act.

Worth a visit: The Anna Bemis Palmer Museum, Lee's Legendary Marble Museum and Wessel's Living History Farm. In Henderson, see Mennonite Heritage Park.

YORK IS THE GEOGRAPHIC CENTER OF THE COUNTY WITH AN ELEVATION OF 1,700 FEET.

ABOUT THE AUTHORS

Dean B. Settle

Dean and his wife, Harriet, spent 35 years together in downtown Lincoln, where they were devoted partners in both life and work. Originally from Iowa, Dean earned his bachelor's and master's degrees from the University of Northern Iowa and pursued postgraduate studies at the University of Wisconsin and DePaul University. Over a distinguished 51-year career in behavioral health, Dean worked across Iowa, Kansas and California before moving to Nebraska in 1989. He managed extensive systems of care, including hospitals and clinics at state and county levels, and was actively involved in state and national rehabilitation associations. For 37 years, he served as a surveyor for the Commission on Accreditation of Rehabilitation Facilities (CARF). A passionate art collector and former gallery owner, Dean has published several books and articles throughout his career. His research for this book allowed him to reconnect with Nebraska's county officials and explore the state's rich architectural history.

Harriet R. Grossbart

Born in New York and raised in South Miami, Harriet graduated from the University of Florida before moving to Nebraska in 1972 to work for Lancaster County. Her career was dedicated to supporting individuals with developmental disabilities, serving as a teacher, administrator and advocate. After retiring, Harriet co-founded a significant payee service company and played a key role in developing a foundation that manages special needs trusts. She also wrote legislation and manuals and contributed to professional journals. An avid traveler, Harriet cherished both domestic and international trips, with Spain being a particular favorite. In her adopted state of Nebraska, she delighted in exploring small towns and unwinding in the Sand Hills. Harriet passed away in November 2023 from cancer, leaving a legacy of advocacy and a final wish for her husband to complete this passion project.

CONTRIBUTORS

EDITOR • Chris Christen

Chris Christen brings extensive journalism experience to this project as a contributing researcher, writer and editor. Since transitioning from newspapers to public relations and communications in 2021, she has embraced book editing and publishing as a side pursuit, with a particular passion for historical themes. A chance meeting at a mutual friend's book signing in Lincoln in early 2024 led to her collaboration with Dean on this book.

DESIGNER • Christine Zueck-Watkins

Christine Zueck-Watkins is an accomplished book designer with 60 titles to her credit, spanning companies, nonprofits and individuals. Her expertise has earned her notable recognition, including a Best Non-Fiction Award from the Nebraska Center for the Book. Christine also has extensive experience in photo retouching and restoration.

PHOTOGRAPHY
Dean B. Settle
Kurt A. Keeler
Chris Christen
Ed Sexton
Berggren Architects, P.C.

PROOFREADERS
Kurt A. Keeler
Carole Levin

ILLUSTRATIONS
Mike Parks, courtesy Omaha World-Herald

SPECIAL THANKS
Allen J. Beermann
Jerry Berggren
Peggy Birky
Erin Dobesh
Nancy Finkin
Kim Hawley
Keith Larsen
Megan McCollister
Candace Meredith
Hilary Roit
Ed Sexton
Corey Steel
Mike Tobias

www.ingramcontent.com/pod-product-compliance
Lightning Source LLC
Chambersburg PA
CBHW080912170426
43201CB00017B/2303